MARRIAGE WITH MEANING

A Values-Based Model for Premarital Counseling

RABBI DANIEL YOUNG

iUniverse, Inc.
Bloomington

Marriage with Meaning
A Values-Based Model for Premarital Counseling

iUniverse books may be ordered through booksellers or by contacting:

iUniverse
1663 Liberty Drive
Bloomington, IN 47403
www.iuniverse.com
1-800-Authors (1-800-288-4677)

Because of the dynamic nature of the Internet, any Web addresses or links contained in this book may have changed since publication and may no longer be valid. The views expressed in this work are solely those of the author and do not necessarily reflect the views of the publisher, and the publisher hereby disclaims any responsibility for them.

ISBN: 978-1-4502-6111-1 (sc)
ISBN: 978-1-4502-6112-8 (ebook)

Printed in the United States of America

iUniverse rev. date: 12/17/2010

In appreciation of:
Richard Levy for guiding the initial research for this project.
Ann and Richard Young for supporting this work.
Beth Young for believing in this project and helping make it a reality.

Table of Contents

Preface   xi

The History of and Case for Premarital Counseling—
A Note for Clergy   xii

Introduction   xv
    Romantic Love and Companionate Love   xvi
    Rationale for this Project   xvii
    Using this Book   xix
    Outline of the Book   xx

Chapter 1:   Planning for Your Big Day   1
    A Note for Same-sex Couples   2
    Well in Advance of the Wedding   2
       Getting the Rabbi   2
       Ketubah   3
       Chupah   3
       Rings   4
       Marriage License   4
    Before the Wedding   5
       Aufruf   5
       Mikvah   5
       Separation   7
       Fasting   7
       Kabbalat Panim/Tisch   7
       Signing the Ketubah   8
       Bedeken   8
    The Ceremony   10
       Processional   10
       Circling   11
       Birkat Eirusin   11
       Vows   12
       Sheva Brachot   13
       Breaking the Glass   14
       Recessional-Yichud   15
       Additional Readings   16

Conclusion   16
Checklist for Wedding Day   16
Review—Places to Honor Friends and Family   16

Chapter 2:   Who You Are and Who You Want to Become   18
Reflecting on the Past   19
  Exploring Family Love   20
The First Task of Marriage   23
Changing Relationships with Family and Friends   26
In-Laws   27
A Look to the Future   30
Beginning to Dream   32
Finding Your Place in the Chain of *Dorot*   35

Chapter 3:   Communication and Conflict in Intimate Relationships 36
Who?   37
What?   39
Where?   42
When?   43
Why?   45
How?   46
  Communication Techniques   46
  Conflict Resolution   49
  Children and Conflict   53
  Repair Attempts   54
  A Word about Violence and Abuse   56
Wrapping It Up   56

Chapter 4:   Investing in Your Marriage   57
Day-to-Day Living   59
  Your Views of Money   59
  Responsibility for Money Matters   61
  Income vs. Expenses   63
  Keeping a Positive Balance in the Emotional Bank Account   64
The Short-Term   66
  Planning Beyond Today: Finances for the Short-Term   66
  Allowing Your Relationship to Grow   68
  52 Ways to Work on Your Marriage   70
  The Sentence-Completion Game   72
The Long-Term   73
  Financial Planning for the Long-Term   73
  Emotional Bank Account: Long-Term   74
  Conclusion   76

Chapter 5:   Building a Fulfilling and Successful Home Life   77
   Chores   78
   Sexual Intimacy   81
     Good Sex   82
     Ethical Sex   83
     A Voice from Tradition   85
     Sexual Problems   86
     Infidelity   86
     A Closing Exercise   89
   Children   90
     Jewish Genetic Testing   93
     Infertility   93
   Religious Observance   94
     Heavenly Thoughts   96
     Trying New Rituals   99
   Conclusion   100

Chapter 6:   Tying it All Together   101
   Putting the Value of *Dorot* into Your Ceremony   103
   Including the Value of *Dorot* in Your New Marriage   104
   Putting the Values of *Emet* and *Emunah* into Your Ceremony   104
   Including the Values of *Emet* and *Emunah* in Your New Marriage   105
   Putting the Value of *Acharayut* into Your Ceremony   105
   Including the Value of *Acharayut* in Your New Marriage   106
   Putting the Value of *Bayit* into Your Ceremony   106
   Including the Value of *Bayit* in Your New Marriage   107

Bibliography   109

Endnotes   121

Preface

Two comments must be made at the outset that will affect how some of you read this manual. First of all, we must recognize that some texts of older vintage do not reflect the same sensibilities as our modern age. Some sources used in this manual, particularly the ancient Jewish texts, are from times before gender-neutral language—times when there *were* defined roles for men and women in a society. As such, these texts may use language different from that to which we are accustomed. I have chosen to let the texts speak in the original, recognizing that many of them could be modernized. Despite the gender-role assumptions in many of these texts, they still provide relevant and important insights into marriage. Therefore, when not quoting other sources, this manual will use inclusive terms such as "partner" instead of "man/husband" or "woman/wife" since it is designed for use by all couples seeking to enter into a sacred covenant with each other.

Furthermore, most of the texts used in this manual assume a heterosexual union. Quite simply, this is because all of the marriage literature published in generations past—and most today—assumes a heterosexual union. However, I believe that this manual has relevant and important things to say to same-sex couples as well. Research has shown that "the processes of close relationships are very similar in heterosexual and homosexual couples."[1] That does not mean that there are no differences in the issues that heterosexual couples face and same-sex couples face. Same-sex couples often need to deal with family reactions, community reactions, and legal issues that heterosexual couples do not. I hope that the skills presented in this manual give couples the tools to begin to constructively deal with those issues together.

The History of and Case for Premarital Counseling—A Note for Clergy

Premarital counseling is an ever-evolving craft. Rabbis and social workers have long been interested in determining the best way to influence young couples and increase their chances for a successful marriage. In the 1930s, the Reform rabbinical association, the Central Conference of American Rabbis (CCAR), created a new committee to develop guidelines for rabbinic premarital counseling:

> In June 1936, upon the initiative of Rabbi Sidney E. Goldstein, the CCAR committee on Marriage, Family, and the Home was created. This committee recommended that "each synagogue should develop a program to include premarital conferences in which every young couple shall before marriage be instructed in the meaning of marriage and the foundations of the family in accordance with both Jewish ideals and the conclusions of current social science."[2]

This sounds rather reasonable. The leaders of the Reform movement seem to have taken these guidelines seriously. In the 1950s, the suggested premarital counseling program looked like this:

> The most common religious program falls under the category of "individual counseling." A series of four individual sessions may be held. The first session could last for one hour and focus on the purpose of the entire interview program, details of the ceremony, clarification of

state laws, and distribution of literature. Many counseling programs end at this point. It is advisable, however, to see the couple for a second session that lasts one to one and one-half hours. During that time, the meaning of marriage could be discussed and a sex-knowledge inventory known as "Form X" administered. This test is reviewed during the third session. The last interview would cover the spiritual aspects of marriage and close with a prayer.[3]

This plan is consistent with the results of a survey conducted by the CCAR near the middle of the last century in which 77 percent of respondents reported counseling couples over and above any conversations about the wedding ceremony. The average time rabbis spent with couples preparing for marriage was 1.68 hours.

A generation later, the amount of time spent preparing a couple for marriage was contrasted with the amount of time a rabbi spent preparing for other life cycle transitions:

A busy rabbi has more than he can handle in just arranging for the wedding ceremony. Yet, there is something disproportionate here. For pastoral work in connection with, say, the death of a congregant, the rabbi devotes several hours to helping the family before, during, and after the funeral. But in preparation "for life," for marriage, with its profound consequences to the lives of so many people, the rabbi limits himself to the brief hour, if that much, of pre-ceremony consultation. Surely marriage, and marriage in these days of social upheaval, deserves a reordering of priorities.[4]

Not only is the limited time in premarital counseling a question of priorities, it is also a missed opportunity. Helping couples prepare for marriage has the potential to make a big difference. Facilitating constructive conversations and helping create healthy patterns can pay off for the couple down the road:

More than in any other area of the "helping-people art," the clergyman is in an ideal position in which one can help couples take constructive steps at the beginning of the marriage. Couples do come to clergymen to be married, and they can utilize this opportunity to do an important task in the education for marriage. Two or three hours spent with a couple in a premarital counseling interview can do more than ten hours of marriage counseling after the conflicts and hostilities have seared the victims and done the damage.[5]

The importance of premarital counseling has only grown in the intervening years, as we have become more aware of the complexities of marriage. We might even say that marriage is a more complicated venture than it was a generation or two ago, as many more issues are being discussed and decided by today's couples. Where a generation ago, it might have been assumed that the couple would have children, today we recognize that not all couples want children (or are able to have them). Where a generation ago, it might have been assumed that the woman would stay at home with the children, today we recognize that either parent might take on that role or that neither parent might, instead trusting the child to the care of a nanny or daycare.

As a result, it is important to have a premarital program that allows couples to begin to probe these challenging topics in a safe and supportive environment. This manual is written as a guide to the important conversations that couples should have before they get married. It is written to speak directly to the couple. Reading it yourself will, however, provide you with a way to structure your own premarital counseling and enable you to call the couple's attention to particular sections that you think will be meaningful for them.

When we invite couples on this journey of premarital counseling, we truly become *m'sadrei kiddushin*—the term can mean much more than just arranging and performing the couple's wedding ceremony. It is an invitation to us as *k'lei kodesh* to communicate the sanctity of the couple's individual marital union and help them unlock marriage's potential.

This manual is an invitation to rabbis and couples to take this moment of transition seriously, equipping couples with tools for finding meaning and fulfillment in their marriage.

Introduction

The decision to get married is a big one and it is not one that should be taken lightly. The two of you have decided to make a very serious commitment to one another and are to be congratulated for doing so. Coming to the conclusion that your partner is the person with whom you want to spend the rest of your life is not easy. So much of what we value in life is choice. With marriage, you are saying that you are relinquishing your choice to date other people for the opportunity to spend the rest of your life with your partner.

For prior generations, marriage was not as much a choice as it was an expectation. "Once upon a time, everybody got married, usually soon after they left college, and happy or sad, they were likely to stay with those partners. Pregnant people felt they *had* to get married, and cohabitation was known as living in sin. But not so anymore. Marriage is now a *choice*."[6] The two of you are choosing marriage as the way to sanctify your relationship. In making this choice, a whole new world of depth and meaning opens up to you.

It's a good thing that we have marriage, for "what we need, and need desperately, is a protected inner world in which we can take off our masks, relax, and learn to develop our hidden potential as loving, caring persons."[7] This close connection of marriage made safe by the commitment that we make to one another allows us to grow to understand ourselves and to become intimately connected with another person. In short, "marriage provides an oasis where sex, humor, and play can flourish."[8]

But, marriage is not easy. "We do not see Prince Charming and Cinderella on to their honeymoon bed because all the fairy tales end at the altar. After that, the plot grows too hard to follow."[9] Part of this challenge of marriage comes from the transition from an individual model to a team model. "In relationships, there is never really one winner and one loser; two people either win—or lose—together."[10] When a couple succeeds in forming a team, love flourishes and the two individuals grow to be stronger and better people than either could have become alone. As we learn in Ecclesiastes Rabbah 4, "Husband and wife together are greater as a unit than each of them is as an individual."[11]

Successfully navigating life together means becoming attuned to the complexity of sharing a life together. It means expending energy and effort to create a relationship of mutual understanding and respect, a place where intimacy can flourish. A good marriage requires considerable and consistent effort—it doesn't just happen on its own.

Romantic Love and Companionate Love

We often speak of "falling in love." The moment of falling in love suggested to you that this relationship with your partner was no ordinary friendship— there was the possibility of much more. Yet, as Michael Kaufman notes, this idea of falling in love does not accurately express love's role in a caring, committed relationship:

> [O]ne does not *fall* into genuine love; one *grows* into it. The learning process of understanding the other's personality and becoming aware of the other's interests and needs is slow and difficult. It is far removed from the instant, effortless sensation that "falling in love" implies. Love that is based upon the solid foundations of friendship, affection, empathy, reciprocal giving, knowledge, and understanding is sure to be more enduring.[12]

You, near the beginning of the life you hope to build together, are just seeing the beginning of what your love can grow to be. A Biblical example serves to illustrate this point. "Scripture tells us first that Isaac married Rebecca—and only then are we informed that he loved her. The affection that abides between a couple before [marriage] may indeed be genuine, but the deep and lasting love based on knowledge comes only through living and growing together in marriage."[13]

The idea of marrying for love is relatively new. In centuries past, political, economic, practical, and familial reasons all trumped love as a factor in choosing a mate. It is different today. Today, love is an essential component of what brings people to marry each other. Yet, research shows that this love is different from the love that sustains them through the course of their marriage. The love that attracts people to each other is what we might label romantic love or, in a word, passion. Yet according to relationship research, the passion that a couple feels as they date and prepare to marry is not what will sustain them throughout their lives together. So, if passion isn't what sustains most successful long-term relationships, what does? Couples who have happy, successful marriages establish a relationship of genuine friendship with each other: "Each is the other's best friend. The prophet Malachi refers to a wife as 'your friend (companion) and the wife of your covenant.'"[14] Companionate love—friendship—is what sustains strong and successful relationships. Nothing more and nothing less.

Many couples are surprised when the passion that they experienced so strongly early in their relationship begins to fade. Some couples see this as a signal that something is wrong in their relationship. In reality, research tells us that this is a normal stage in the development of a long-term relationship. Passion simply can't be sustained over a lifetime in the same way that intimacy can. As one researcher notes:

> Enjoy passion, but don't make it the foundation of the relationships that you hope will last. Nurture a friendship with your lover. Try to stay fresh; grab every opportunity to enjoy novel adventures with your spouse... And don't be surprised or disappointed if your urgent desires gradually resolve into placid but deep affection for your beloved. That happy result is likely to make you a lucky lover.[15]

It is therefore essential to cultivate a full and rich relationship—one that thrives on more than passion—because as research shows us, passion is fleeting; companionship and friendship are the keys to the survival of long-term love.

Rationale for this Project

Marriage is a great transition. It is a time when, even if the couple has been living together prior to marriage, two separate lives merge together as one. It is a time of great excitement and great anxiety. Planning for a wedding and a marriage brings up many emotions that can be hard to deal with and many questions to which it is hard to find reliable answers.

Meeting individually with the clergy who will be performing the ceremony is important. The officiant should get to know the couple that he or she will join in marriage and you should get to know your officiant and be comfortable with him or her. It is also important to see that the

Jewish community has something of substance to offer you at this point in your lives. It is my not-so-subtle hope that, through the course of reading this manual and talking with your rabbi or cantor, you will see the Jewish community as a place of comfort and strength and a place where you will choose to be involved.

Engaging in a program of premarital preparation has clear benefits. One positive is that, "Life cycle crises are a time for great personal growth. The more people do to prepare for something, the stronger the commitment. The same can be said for marriage preparation."[16] You might not think of your marriage as a "crisis," but it does mean a radical intensification of your relationship and a change in the way you are seen by the outside world. Therefore, the more seriously you take marriage and the preparation for it, the more likely you are to work to create the meaning in marriage that we all wish for you as you stand under the *chuppah*.

Premarital counseling can also diffuse some issues that might have become bigger ones later in the relationship just by putting them on the table at such a formative moment your relationship. But, premarital counseling will not solve all the challenges you might encounter. There may still be a time that you face substantial difficulty and need to look for help. A good premarital counseling program will validate this statement from the 1950s: "In a sense, we may consider this premarital interview as a pre-counseling contract, which prepares the way for real counseling when it is needed."[17] If premarital counseling does nothing more than suggest that marriage counseling is not taboo at a time when it becomes necessary, it has served an important purpose in helping you to succeed in marriage.

With all this, it is important to note that this program of premarital counseling is not the ideal. Research has shown that the best time to have these conversations about the opportunities and challenges of marriage is six months *after* your wedding. In order to get the most benefit out of this manual, it is best to come back to it several months after your wedding when you have an understanding of your marriage's strengths and weaknesses.

Premarital counseling lays the foundation for you to have important conversations and reflect on your counseling sessions as a way to deal with the difficult adjustment to marriage. Throughout the course of this book, you will have the opportunity to learn more about yourself and your partner; you will continue to develop your identity as a couple; you will learn values that can guide you throughout your married life; and, in this book, you will have a resource to which you can refer in difficult times.

Some may wonder why it is important to have a book written from a Jewish perspective. What can ancient texts offer that social science cannot? Much of the social science literature on marriage—and certainly the articles and books that are still widely read—were published within the last hundred years. Studies are done constantly that reveal aspects of human relationships. The field of social science—as it relates to the study of relationships—is constantly evolving. Jewish tradition offers a different perspective—that of history. Jews have gotten married throughout three-thousand-year history of the Jewish people's existence. Over this long span, Jewish authors have learned about love and marriage as well. They learn not by looking at the latest research, but by looking at the relationship between the two lovers. By merging social science with Jewish tradition, we have the best of both worlds—a theoretically sound counseling model rooted in the experience and wisdom of tradition.

A further benefit to this manual on marriage from the Jewish perspective is the ability to use Jewish values to frame the discussion. Each of the final five chapters of the manual Chapters 2–5 utilize Jewish values to help frame and deepen the discussion of the topic. Each chapter introduces a Jewish value or two that will highlight the chapter's themes. I hope that you find these values compelling and choose to make them the foundation upon which your relationship rests.

The goals of the coming chapters are neatly summed up by Rabbi Ellen Lewis: "The process involved in achieving emotional and spiritual preparation for marriage is threefold: (1) to help the couple feel comfortable talking about emotional issues with a third party; (2) to help them communicate effectively with each other; and (3) to do both of these in a Jewish context."[18]

Using this Book

This book is designed to be used as a companion for a five-session program of rabbinic premarital counseling or as a text for couples to read and consider on their own.

This introduction and the next chapter are introductory materials to be read outside of the five-session counseling program. This introduction sets the stage for all that follows and the first chapter begins the conversation of what the couple wants the ceremony to look like. It is organized in this way because there are several issues that the couple will need to begin working on long before the wedding, such as selecting a *ketubah* and wedding rings. Leaving these important items until the last chapter would not leave the couple enough time to take care of them in advance of the wedding.

The five sessions begin in Chapter 2 and continue through Chapter 6. Each of the chapters is designed to be a companion for a conversation and reflection on important issues in your young relationship. The last chapter, which would be the last session, is the time for planning out the details of the actual ceremony. Planning the ceremony is intentionally left for the end of this manual for a couple of reasons:

1. The values that are discussed throughout the manual will shape what you decide to include in your ceremony.
2. Learning how to be married is more vital to your long-term success as a married couple than the wedding ceremony.

Outline of the Book

In the pages that follow, you will have the opportunity to consider what marriage means to you. You will be prompted to have conversations about your expectations of marriage—and you will learn techniques to help make your marriage successful. Many of the issues that social workers and clergy agree are important to laying the foundation for a successful marriage are raised through the rest of this manual through the interplay of secular books on love and marriage and Jewish books and sacred texts.

In Chapter 1, we begin the conversation of what your wedding ceremony will look like. There are many decisions that you—as a couple—will have to make. Among them are choices about whether to include certain rituals in your wedding ceremony and how many people you'd like to have involved in your ceremony and in what ways. Your wedding ceremony is your first chance to make a statement about what is important to you as a married couple. This book will give you the tools to begin to figure out your most important values and to encourage you to use those values to inform how you structure your wedding ceremony and your life together.

The second chapter encourages each of you to reflect on the marriages you observed as you were growing up. If your parents were married—or divorced—what lessons did you learn from them? What legacies do these marriages leave for you? How might what you observed and learned from these marriages influence your marriage? It is important to be aware of these significant issues. Many people think that their marriage involves only the two of them, but in reality, when we enter a marriage, we bring with us our parents' relationship(s) and our past hurts. The more attuned to these influences we are, the better we will understand ourselves and the better our partner will be able to understand us.

Chapter 3 deals with the very important issue of communication. Learning how to talk to your partner in a respectful and constructive way and learning how to listen to what your partner is trying to say to you are two of the most important keys to a successful marriage. Additionally, this chapter deals with how to fight in a constructive manner so that each person's dignity is preserved. "Happily married husbands and wives get depressed, fight, lose jobs, struggle with the demands of the workplace and the crises of infants and teenagers, and confront sexual problems. They cry and yell and get frustrated."[19] This chapter will help you deal with these inevitable conflicts and use them to help your relationship grow.

The fourth chapter deals with your emotional and financial bank accounts. This chapter helps you consider important information about merging two separate financial pictures into one joint portfolio. The metaphor of the bank account is then used as a way of discussing techniques to help you deepen your relationship through emotional intimacy by caring for each other and supporting each other. This is necessary because knowing that you are loved and cherished by your partner is one of the greatest gifts in the world and allows your relationship to remain strong and healthy.

In Chapter 5, the issues of your home life as a couple are addressed. How do you create a home that both of you contribute to building? How do you negotiate a sex relationship that respects both of your wishes in the bedroom? "People mistakenly assume that because couples nowadays enter marriage with sexual experience, building a sexual relationship requires no special attention; given two healthy people, it just happens. But in truth, the new sexual freedom means that people today have much higher expectations. They expect more from themselves and from their partners."[20] You will also have the opportunity to discuss whether or not you want to have children. The chapter will also ask you to consider what kind of ritual observance you want to have in your home. This is an important issue to consider on its own merits, but it will also be used to demonstrate the connection between ritual observance and a healthy relationship. For example, Shabbat can be an important time for you to set aside to renew and reflect on your week and on your relationship. The main point of this chapter is that a good home life does not happen by accident; it is the result of careful discussion and planning.

The final chapter returns to the wedding ceremony. After learning about yourself and your relationship, it is time to make sure that those things that are important to you are reflected in your wedding ceremony. I hope that at the end of that chapter and this manual, you feel well prepared for the adventure of marriage and more in love with your partner than ever!

Two quotations set the tone for what follows in this manual. In Chapter 3 of the *Igeret HaKodesh*, an anonymous text from the middle ages that deals largely with the physical relationship between a man and his wife, we find the following quotation: "All organs of the body are neutral … How man *uses* them determines whether they are holy or profane."[21] In beginning the conversation about making marriage meaningful and successful, we can understand this text's wisdom to remind us that we need to use our hearts, minds, and sexual organs to achieve the holy purpose of a caring and loving marriage.

As we go forth into more specifics about building a strong marriage, it is also wise to keep in mind the following quotation from the Talmud (Kiddushin 40b and Bava Kama 17a): *Talmud gadol, she'hatalmud mayvi liday ma'aseh*—"Study is important, for learning leads to action." I pray that what this manual presents be more than just information. I pray that it makes you more conscious of your behavior in this precious relationship and leads you to act to unlock your marriage's potential and make it into the best love it can be.

Chapter 1:
Planning for Your Big Day

As your wedding day approaches, perhaps you feel excited, ready to begin your new life with your partner; perhaps you are nervous, realizing what a serious commitment marriage is. Perhaps you're enjoying planning your wedding; perhaps you can't wait for the wedding, with all its stresses, to be over. Most likely, you feel some mix of all of these emotions.

Weddings are times that bring out the best and worst in people. There is the joy of seeing two people in love pledging to enter into a covenantal relationship with each other. There is also the sadness that comes with the impending changes in relationships with other people and the memories of those who have died or thoughts of those unable to attend the wedding.

Jewish tradition teaches that a once incomplete person finds completeness by marrying their beloved. According to the Talmud (Sanhedrin 22a), your wedding day culminates a process that began forty days before your conception when an angel called out and said that you would one day marry this particular person. Whether you resonate to that particular rabbinic image or not, it is clear that your wedding day is truly momentous.

On the other hand, it is important to remember that the wedding is just a kickoff to your marriage. If you feel stressed, try to keep in mind that "the wedding is *not* your marriage. Your marriage is the daily living of your loving relationship as you go about the task of creating a life together. The wedding is simply the ceremony that you share with your family and friends to announce your love and commitment to each other, and your intention to spend your life together in the special sanctified relationship."[22] It is the day that you are able to say to those who love you, "This is the person I love and we have chosen to spend the rest of our lives together!"

1

There are many rituals in a Jewish marriage that we will now consider. They fall into three basic categories:

- Things that you will need to take care of quite early on in your wedding preparations to make sure that you have what you want by the time the wedding takes place.
- Jewish options that help you prepare for your marriage.
- Parts of the wedding ceremony—explaining what the required parts of a Jewish wedding are and where there is room for you to make choices.

It is worth noting that this chapter will not deal with any of the arrangements for a reception that might follow your wedding. There are countless books that will help you with that should you want to avail yourselves of them. It is important, however, to have a reception that reflects values that are important to you. Some of those values will be things that we will discuss in this manual, so while we will be talking about creating a strong marriage, feel free to use what you learn about marriage and each other to help you plan your reception.

A Note for Same-sex Couples

The remainder of this chapter details the traditional Jewish wedding ceremony and its adaptations for modern times. In creating wedding ceremonies for same-sex couples, some rabbis use a variation of this ceremony—with major or minor changes. Some couples and clergy prefer to use a different ceremony entirely. Because there is so much variance in practice, same-sex wedding ceremonies are not treated in this work. It is worth reading this chapter to understand traditional Jewish wedding practices for potential use or adaptation in your own ceremony, but the language for the rest of this chapter will be based on the heterosexual marriage model since that is the tradition that we inherited from our ancestors.

Well in Advance of the Wedding

Getting the Rabbi

As soon as you get engaged (or in relatively short order after that) it is customary to decide on a date and make arrangements with a rabbi.[23]

If there is a specific rabbi you would like to conduct your wedding, it is appropriate to speak with him or her before committing to a date. Once you know when the rabbi is available, you can proceed to secure a time and place for your wedding. If you are not partial to who conducts your wedding ceremony, you can find a place, choose a date, and see which rabbi is available on that date. Keep in mind that many rabbis' calendars fill up several months in advance, so you are well advised to work quickly to find a rabbi to officiate at your wedding.

Ketubah

You should also begin looking for a *ketubah*. A *ketubah* is a Jewish marriage contract whose history dates back well over two thousand years. It originated as a progressive attempt by Jewish tradition to provide for the rights of women in the event of divorce or death of their spouse. The *ketubah* specified what the wife would inherit in the event of the dissolution of her marriage. These protections prevented the man's sons (some of whom might be from a relationship with another woman) from keeping the entire inheritance.

In modern times, the *ketubah* has been reinterpreted. Instead of a document detailing the financial arrangements of the marriage, the *ketubah*—as used in modern, liberal circles—now reflects some of the promises and values of the couple getting married. As a result, many different texts are available for a *ketubah*.

In an effort to make the *ketubah* a document that doesn't just get filed away somewhere never to be looked at again, many *ketubot* (the plural of *ketubah*) are elaborately decorated with the intention of being framed and displayed in people's homes. Some people commission a *ketubah* from an artist to be designed especially for them; some find a design and a text they like from the local Jewish bookstore or online; and some choose to use a simple piece of paper that may or may not be displayed in their home. Of course, the cost associated with these options varies greatly. The clergyperson doing your wedding can help you locate a *ketubah* that you will find both beautiful and meaningful.

Chupah

Another feature of a Jewish wedding is a *chupah*. The *chupah* is the canopy under which the couple stands. Open on all sides, the *chupah* reminds us of the hospitality of Abraham and Sarah who generously welcomed strangers into their home. Its openness expresses the hope that your home be open to the outside world. Judaism places a high value on *hachnasat orchim*, welcoming the stranger, and it is hoped that your home will be a place that is welcoming to family, friends, and those in need. Yet a *chupah* is also a covered structure. By providing an element of privacy and protection, the *chupah* reminds you that it is also important to have and to cherish your own private space. The *chupah*, then, is symbolic of one of the great tasks that the two of you will have to negotiate: finding the balance between being connected to the outside world and carving out your own personal, private, and protected space. This topic will be addressed more fully in a later chapter.

A Sephardic custom (originating in Jewish communities in Spain and the Middle East), and the custom in Israel, is to use a large *tallit* (prayer shawl) as the top of the canopy. Others use a precious family linen or cloth with symbolic meaning. Some have chosen to have their guests or other important people in their lives decorate squares that then are sewn together to make their c*hupah*, which is then often displayed in the couple's new home. Often, your synagogue will have a *chupah* you can use or be able to locate one for you.

Four poles are attached to the top of the *chupah* at the corners. These poles may be freestanding or they may need to be held. Because of its symbolism, being asked to hold the *chupah* is a great honor.

Rings

In Jewish tradition, the marriage is enacted through an exchange, in the presence of witnesses, of an item of value given for the purpose of marriage. This is customarily done through the use of a wedding ring. Jewish wedding rings are bands of solid metal, containing no stones, but may be engraved, "A band made of a single pure metal, with no holes breaking the circle, represents the wholeness achieved through marriage and a hope for an unbroken union."[24]

Marriage License

In order for a marriage to be recognized by the state and the government, you need to have a signed marriage license. The license is something that you need to apply for and pick up in advance of your wedding. It is signed on the day of your wedding and returned to the state. If you do not know whom to contact, your rabbi can help you get in touch with the appropriate officials. It is important to initiate the process so that you have the required paperwork in time for your wedding!

Before the Wedding

All of the customs that follow in this section are presented as options. It is up to you, your partner, and the rabbi to decide which, if any, you will incorporate. These traditions enriched the marriages of generations of Jews and should be given serious consideration by the two of you.

Aufruf

It is customary on the Shabbat before the wedding (although many choose to celebrate the *aufruf*, a Yiddish word meaning "called up," a week or two before the wedding) for the groom to be called to the Torah for an *aliyah* (to recite the blessings before and after the reading of Torah). In many liberal synagogues, the bride and groom are called up together. Another option, popular in liberal synagogues, is for the couple to come up for a special blessing as the time for their wedding approaches. It is a nice way to share your wedding with your synagogue community and to get their good wishes as you prepare for your big day!

Mikvah

In the days leading up to the wedding, some choose to go to the *mikvah*, the Jewish ritual bath. The *mikvah* is a millennia-old tradition of achieving spiritual cleanliness and a new beginning. A person goes to the *mikvah* already physically clean—having showered and not wearing makeup, nail polish, or any other sort of adornments. The purpose of the *mikvah* is to provide a spiritual cleansing:

> For brides and grooms, *mikvah* is a physical enactment of the passage from being unmarried to married. Entering the *huppah* is a public declaration of a change in status; entering the *mikvah* is a private transforming moment. Metaphorically, immersion creates newborns—virgins— so *mikvah* can be seen as the demarcation between premarital and married sexuality.
>
> A *mikvah* is any body of *mayim hayyim*, literally, "living water," running water as opposed to stagnant water. Ponds, lakes, rivers, and seas are natural *mikvaot*. For many, *mikvah* in a body of natural water is a more satisfying experience—spiritually, emotionally, and aesthetically—

5

than *mikvah* indoors in what looks like a miniature swimming pool. However, weather or climate or family custom often discourages outdoor *mikvah*.[25]

Marriage is a new beginning, a start of a new chapter in your lives. Going to the *mikvah* can help prepare you for this dramatic, exciting transition.

Mikvah is done by immersing yourself entirely in a body of water, so that no part of your body is in contact with any surface. Your hair should be fully submerged as well. In enclosed *mikvaot*, the immersion is done while naked so as to provide the most contact with the purifying water as possible. At these enclosed *mikvaot*, as opposed to natural sources of water, there is an attendant to help you through the procedure. Friends and loved ones of the opposite gender are welcome to attend the *mikvah*, and are asked to wait outside while the immersion takes place.

At least two immersions are customary. After the first immersion, it is appropriate to recite the following blessing:

בָּרוּךְ אַתָּה יְיָ, אֱלֹהֵינוּ מֶלֶךְ הָעוֹלָם אֲשֶׁר קִדְּשָׁנוּ בְּמִצְוֹתָיו, וְצִוָּנוּ עַל הַטְבִילָה.

Baruch Atah Adonai, Eloheinu Melech Haolam, asher kidshanu b'mitzvotav v'tzivanu al hat'vilah.

Blessed are you, Adonai our God, Ruler of the universe, who has commanded us regarding immersion.

Some also include the *Shehecheyanu*:

בָּרוּךְ אַתָּה יְיָ, אֱלֹהֵינוּ מֶלֶךְ הָעוֹלָם, שֶׁהֶחֱיָנוּ וְקִיְּמָנוּ וְהִגִּיעָנוּ לַזְּמַן הַזֶּה.

Baruch Atah Adonai, Eloheinu Melech Haolam, shehecheyanu, v'kiy'manu v'higiyanu laz'man hazeh.

Blessed are You, Adonai our God, Ruler of the universe for giving us life, for sustaining us and for allowing us to reach this moment.

Separation

Some observe the custom of remaining separate from one's betrothed for the day leading up to the wedding. Others remain separated for up to a week prior to the wedding. While you are making a pledge to join a partnership, a brief period of separation reminds you that you are both individuals. The poet Kahlil Gibran says, "Let there be spaces in your togetherness."[26] A further emotional benefit is offered by Maurice Lamm: "It has been suggested that the tradition of separation is only applicable to the day before the wedding to enhance the joy of their meeting as partners."[27] This short period of separation allows for a reunion on the wedding day that makes the experience all the more intense.

A practical consideration in this decision is figuring out when photographs are to take place. If the two of you have been separate, you may decide to come together for photographs before the wedding so as to be able to enjoy the reception after the wedding without worrying about gathering friends and family for pictures. Many couples who choose to observe the custom of separation will take all the pictures that can be taken with just one of them before the wedding and save only those for which both partners are needed until after the wedding, thereby reducing the photography time and allowing more time to celebrate.

Fasting

Another custom that some observe is to fast on the wedding day until the ceremony concludes. Jewish tradition views one's wedding day as a miniature Yom Kippur—a time for reflection and renewal of body and spirit. It is no coincidence therefore that many observant Jews will go to the *mikvah* before Yom Kippur as well as before their weddings. As with any Jewish ritual practice, fasting should only be practiced if it will not put your health or well-being at risk—or even interfere with your ability to truly be present at this moment in your life.

Kabbalat Panim/Tisch

It is becoming increasingly popular in liberal circles to recover ancient traditions for the moments leading up to the wedding. The first of these (chronologically) is *kabbalat panim* or the *tisch*. *Kabbalat panim* literally means "the receiving of faces." It is customary to have the women gather together (either all the women invited or a close circle of family and friends) to sing, tell jokes, and otherwise amuse the bride. The men, on the other hand, are participating in a *tisch*, Yiddish for "table." In the groom's *tisch*, the groom attempts to teach something from the weekly Torah portion. It is the job of the others present to interrupt his teaching with song and dance thereby filling the last moments before the wedding begins with song and laughter. As liberal Jews reclaim these traditions, it is perfectly appropriate to adapt them to best suit the two of you. Perhaps both of you want to do *tisches*—or perhaps you both want to do *kabbalat panim*. If you have decided not to remain separate from each other on the day before the wedding, it is possible to do a joint *tisch* with one or both partners teaching.

Signing the Ketubah

Immediately before the ceremony begins, it is time to sign the *ketubah*. Two witnesses are asked to sign the *ketubah* along with the bride, groom, and officiant. Out of a concern that family members might have ulterior motives in ensuring the marriage takes place, Jewish tradition has held that the witnesses should not be related by blood to either the bride or the groom. Since the ketubah is a Jewish legal document, typically those who serve as witnesses are Jews.

    Halacha, Jewish law, imposes stricter conditions on who may and may not serve as a witness. According to *halacha*, the witnesses must be male and also be ritually observant (often defined by observing all of the Shabbat prohibitions proscribed in Jewish law, known in Hebrew as being *shomer Shabbat*). Some who are concerned with *halacha*, but also committed to equality among the genders will invite four witnesses—two men and two women—to satisfy the *halachic* requirements and involve both men and women.

Bedeken

Bedeken is the custom of the groom lowering his bride's veil just before the ceremony begins. The use of a veil dates back to Biblical times; its first mention occurred at the initial meeting of Rebecca and Isaac:

> And Isaac went out walking in the field toward evening and, looking up, he saw camels approaching. Raising her eyes, Rebecca saw Isaac. She alighted from the camel and said to the servant, "Who is that man walking in the field toward us?" And the servant said, "That is my master." So she took her veil and covered herself. (Genesis 24:63–65)

Although this describes their meeting, because their marriage was arranged, it was also the moment of their wedding.

The custom of the groom lowering the bride's veil comes out of the Biblical story of Jacob as he prepares to marry Rachel. He is in the house of Laban, his uncle, and asks his uncle to give him Rachel's hand in marriage.

> When he had stayed with him a month's time, Laban said to Jacob, "Just because you are a kinsman, should you serve me for nothing? Tell me, what shall your wages be?" Now Laban had two daughters; the name of the older one was Leah, and the name of the younger was Rachel. Leah had weak eyes; Rachel was shapely and beautiful. Jacob loved Rachel; so he answered, "I will serve you seven years for your younger daughter Rachel." Laban said, "Better that I give her to you than that I should give her to an outsider. Stay with me." So Jacob served seven years for Rachel and they seemed to him but a few days because of his love for her.

> Then Jacob said to Laban, "Give me my wife, for my time is fulfilled, that I may cohabit with her." And Laban gathered all the people of the place and made a feast. When evening came, he took his daughter Leah and brought her to him; and he cohabited with her … When morning came, there was Leah! So he said to Laban, "What is this you have done to me? I was in your service for Rachel! Why did you deceive me?" Laban said, "It is not the practice in our place to marry off the younger before the older. "Wait until the bridal week of this one is over and we will give you that one too, provided you serve me another seven years." Jacob did so; he waited out the bridal week of the one and then he gave him his daughter Rachel as wife. (Genesis 29:14b-23, 25-28)

It is because of this story of trickery that the custom developed to have the groom lower the veil of his bride so that there be no confusion about who he was marrying! The word *bedeken* means checking. Once the groom is confident that he has the right bride, we can continue to proceed toward the wedding. Some couples choose to make the *bedeken* ceremony egalitarian by having the bride affix the groom's *kippah* (headcovering) as they prepare to head toward the *chupah*. A *bedeken* ceremony can be done in public or it can be a more private moment shared with the closest family and friends. The decision is yours.

The Ceremony

It is important to note that not all parts of the wedding will be discussed in this section. It is primarily the places in which you—as a couple—will need to make a decision of some sort that might require some research, thought, and conversation between you or places where you might want to ask people to participate. The ceremony will be gone over in its entirety at the last meeting before the wedding.

Processional

Finally, it is time for the wedding. Much of the ordering of the processional—such as whether groomsmen walk down alone or with bridesmaids—is up to you, but there are a few places where order is important. This section will detail those.

1. If either partner has grandparents present at the ceremony, it is customary to have a relative or a member of the bridal party usher them to their seats right before the processional begins.
2. The officiant(s) should be the first members of the procession.
3. It is customary in Jewish weddings for the parent(s) of the bride or groom to escort their child to the *chupah* and to remain at the *chupah* with their child throughout the ceremony.

It is important to be conscious of the choices you make in music for the processional and to share those choices with the rabbi. Many rabbis are not comfortable using the work of the composer Richard Wagner. While a very talented and celebrated musician, he was also known to be an anti-Semite, therefore his music seems inappropriate to many at a Jewish wedding! Others may prefer not to use the "traditional" wedding march by Mendelssohn, instead encouraging different musical choices, perhaps those from Jewish composers or melodies for particular Jewish texts. The same holds true for music during the recessional.

Circling

At a traditional wedding, once the bride arrives at the end of the processional, but before she enters the *chupah*, she will circle the groom seven times. In the mystical tradition, this act symbolizes the bride entering the seven realms of her beloved's soul. Another, less mystical, interpretation is that the circling is meant to symbolize the new family unit that is about to be created between the two of them, separate from parents and everyone else in attendance at the wedding.

Many liberal Jewish weddings do not contain the custom of circling at all. For those that do, often an egalitarian alternative to this ritual is practiced. Instead of the bride circling the groom seven times, one partner walks three circles around the other, and then they switch with the partner who was in the middle of the circle circling his or her beloved three times. The seventh, and last, circle is made by the two partners walking together in a circle, creating their own sacred space.

Birkat Eirusin

If you look at a Jewish wedding ceremony, you will notice that the blessing over the wine appears twice in the wedding service, once quite early on and once during the *Sheva Brachot* (which will be discussed later). This is because the modern Jewish wedding ceremony was once two separate ceremonies. In ancient times, the first half of today's wedding service—*Birkat Eirusin*—came several months before the wedding and marked the couple's betrothal. That meant that the couple was set aside for each other and were considered as married in most matters, but while the arrangements were being finalized, the couple was not permitted to live together. The ceremony that initiated this period was called *Erusin*.

The second ceremony was the marriage ceremony, which transformed their relationship from its semi-permanent status to permanence, called *Nisuin*, or marriage. The couple was now able to live together. A blessing over the wine was offered at this moment as well as part of the *Sheva Brachot*, the seven blessings. Over time, these two ceremonies have merged, so the blessing over the wine appears twice in the wedding service.

This gives you the opportunity to use kiddush cups of your choosing during the ceremony. Your officiant will likely have a kiddush cup if you choose not to use your own—just be sure to inform him/her of your decision. Often, however, there are kiddush cups of sentimental value to the family that a couple would like to use in the service.

Vows

This first section of today's wedding service, *Erusin*, concludes with vows and the exchange of rings. In traditional weddings, only the male says a vow, as in the traditional understanding of marriage, it is the male who is acquiring the female. The male's statement is expressed in the traditional formula *harey at m'kudeshet li b'tabaat zo k'dat Moshe v'Yisrael*— "Behold, you are betrothed to me with this ring according to the laws of Moses and Israel." The one-sided nature of this moment did not sit well with many liberal couples and clergy so in many communities, the other partner also has the opportunity to publicly declare her commitment to her partner through the use of a vow. Some use an altered Hebrew version of the vow the groom makes, *harey ata m'kudash li b'tabaat zo k'dat Moshe v'Yisrael*—"Behold, you are betrothed to me with this ring according to the laws of Moses and Israel." From the traditional perspective, this poses a problem—how can both partners acquire each other? Since the statement, in its ancient understanding, was about acquisition, it would seem to annul the acquisition made by the groom! Liberal authorities dismiss this argument or argue that both partners are making the acquisition, and this formula is still quite popular.

There are, however, alternatives. Some couples use a Biblical text or a text that uses Biblical metaphors, so that the bride can publicly declare her love for her groom. Several options are given here.[28]

אֲנִי לְדוֹדִי וְדוֹדִי לִי.

Ani l'dodi v'dodi li.

I am my beloved's and my beloved is mine. (Song of Songs 6:3)

וְאֵרַשְׂתִּיךְ לִי לְעוֹלָם,
וְאֵרַשְׂתִּיךְ לִי בְּצֶדֶק וּבְמִשְׁפָּט וּבְחֶסֶד וּבְרַחֲמִים.
וְאֵרַשְׂתִּיךְ לִי בֶּאֱמוּנָה וְיָדַעַתְּ אֶת־יְהֹוָה.

V'erastich li l'olam.
V'erastich li b'tzedek uvemishpat, uvechesed uverachamim.
V'erastich li beemunah, v'yadaat et Adonai.

I will betroth you to Me forever.
I will betroth you to Me with righteousness, with justice, with love, and with compassion.
I will betroth you to Me with faithfulness, and you shall know Adonai. (Hosea 2:21–2)

אֲנִי רַעְיָתֵךְ, וְאַתָּה דוֹדִי.

Ani rayatcha, v'atah dodi.

I am your beloved and you are mine.

שִׂימֵנִי כַחוֹתָם עַל־לִבֶּךְ כַּחוֹתָם עַל־זְרוֹעֶךָ

Simeni chachotam al libecha, k'chotam al z'roecha.

Let me be a seal upon your heart, like the seal upon your hand. (Song of Songs 8:6)

It is also perfectly appropriate to write your own vows to share with your spouse on your wedding day. These would be done in addition to the Hebrew vow formulas explained above. It is an opportunity to express the commitment that you are making with the marriage ceremony that you two are celebrating. Having both the traditional words and your modern ones allows you to be connected to the millions of Jewish couples that have come before you and to add your modern voices.[29]

Sheva Brachot

In the second part of the wedding ceremony, *Nisuin*, seven blessings (*Sheva Brachot*) are recited that place the bride and groom in relation to the world that surrounds them. The *Sheva Brachot* begins with the blessing over the second cup of wine used during the wedding ceremony. The wine is not drunk, however, until the conclusion of all seven blessings. The blessings, as you will see, offer thanks and praise for a world in which love exists and can flourish. The series of blessings conclude with the seventh blessing, which praises God for allowing us to celebrate with the bride and groom.

You have a great deal of choice in determining how these blessings are recited in your service. In *The New Jewish Wedding*, Anita Diamant outlines four ideas for how to go about reciting the blessings in your service:

- Read or chanted entirely by the rabbi or cantor
- Read or chanted in Hebrew by the rabbi or cantor with English translations read by designated family members and friends.
- Read by married couples who are asked to share the honor of a blessing: one reading the Hebrew, the other, the English.
- Read or chanted in Hebrew by the rabbi with the English translation read in unison by all the guests, who are given copies of the text.[30]

Most clergy require that those who participate in the reading of the S*heva Brachot* be Jews. Check with your officiant to be sure.

Breaking the Glass

The last moment in the wedding ceremony is a powerful one and the one that for many people is most symbolic of a Jewish wedding. At the end of the ceremony, the groom steps on a glass, shattering it. Some couples like to use special glasses from their family's past at such a momentous occasion. There are companies that will send you a glass to use and then make a ritual object out of the broken glass shards such as a *kiddush* cup or a *mezuzah*. The ritual of breaking the glass has its roots in a Talmudic story (Brachot 31a). "Mar bar Rabina made a marriage feast for his son. He observed that the rabbis present were celebrating extravagantly. So he seized an expensive goblet worth four hundred zuzim and broke it before them. Thus he made them sober." A nice story, but it doesn't explain what the problem was with the rabbis' celebrations. In *The Everything Jewish Wedding Book*, Helen Latner writes:

> What is the significance of breaking the glass? Some rabbis explain it as a reminder that even in happy moments we must be aware of the fragility of life and of all human relationships. Others hold it to be a reminder of the destruction of the Temple in Jerusalem, so that even at the height of rejoicing, we remember this sadness—in fact, all the losses suffered by the Jewish people.

In addition to the quasi-religious interpretations offered for this custom, some people regard the breaking of the glass as a break with childhood, with the parental home and with all other previous liaisons…

A very thin glass is used. To prevent accidents from flying slivers, it is usually placed in … a napkin.[31]

Rabbi Shlomo Carlebach, a famous twentieth-century rabbi and musician, offers us a beautiful understanding of the purpose of the breaking of the glass:

We break a glass to remember Jerusalem. Do you know how much pain we went through for two thousand years to fix Jerusalem, from the day the Romans burned it until 1967 when the Jews once again had access to the whole city? So much, right? So you know what the groom says to his bride right before they leave the chuppah? He says, if God forbid anything gets broken between us, I'm ready to go through that much pain in order to rebuild our home again.

As long as you don't have your soulmate, you're not strong enough to fix the world. When you have a soul mate and a home, you can fix the world. So when you leave the chuppah, you say, "Master of the World, I'm ready. Send all the broken glass to me."[32]

It is with this moment of looking backward and looking forward that the wedding ceremony concludes.

Recessional-Yichud

With the breaking of the glass, your friends and family wish you *mazal tov* and the recessional begins. The newly married couple leaves first followed by the parents (usually the bride's go first). You may then go immediately to a room where you spend your first few moments together as husband and wife in privacy. Especially if you have been fasting, but even if you haven't, it is wise to have a few snacks laid out for you. This time is called *yichud,* which means unity. In ancient times and in traditional circles today, this time would mark the first time that the two of you would have been allowed to be alone together. It is a time for you to unwind, to talk, especially if you haven't seen each other for a period of time, and to bask in the glow of each other's love.

Often people will choose to have a guard or guards outside the room where the couple has *yichud* to ensure their privacy. This is yet another way that you can honor friends or family. After a short while, it is time to emerge and rejoin your guests who will be happy to see you!

Additional Readings

Jewish tradition gives us the outline of the wedding ceremony, but as we have seen, there is plenty of space for you to be creative. Some couples choose to include additional readings to be read by the couple themselves, by their parents, family, or friends, or by the rabbi. If there are any readings you would like to include, be sure to speak with the rabbi in advance.

Conclusion

We will return to the actual wedding ceremony at the end. This chapter is designed to raise issues for you to think about in planning for your ceremony. The next several chapters are devoted to laying the foundation for a happy, healthy, and successful marriage. We will then conclude by returning to planning the wedding ceremony and make sure that your ceremony reflects who you are as a couple and the values that are important in your relationship.

Checklist for Wedding Day

- *Ketubah*
- Pen of the same color ink as used in the *ketubah*
- *Chupah* and poles
- Rings
- *Kiddush* cups (1 or 2)
- Glass to be broken in a napkin
- Marriage license

Review—Places to Honor Friends and Family

- Groomsmen
- Bridesmaids

- *Chupah* holders
- *Ketubah* signers
- Readers of the seven blessings
- Other readings
- *Yichud* guards

Chapter 2:
Who You Are and Who You
Want to Become

The Biblical book of Ecclesiastes teaches, "There is nothing new under the sun" (Ecclesiastes 1:9). This suggests that everything is a repeat or a recreation of what has happened in the past. It might be hard to take Ecclesiastes too seriously in this age of invention, for we have computers, cars, and televisions, all of which rely on technology that has been developed in the last hundred years.

Before we dismiss Ecclesiastes' statement outright, however, we ought to consider that perhaps he wasn't talking about technology. Perhaps he was talking about human nature. Perhaps he was talking about interpersonal relationships, suggesting that we feel the same emotions that people did generations ago. Perhaps he is suggesting that our connections to generations past introduce patterns that play themselves out in future generations. This chapter begins by examining what you have learned from your family and friends that you bring into this relationship and examining how your relationships with family and friends might change with your upcoming marriage. The chapter concludes with a conversation about goal setting, encouraging you to consider how you might make your relationship a strong one, as well as a good role model for the next generation.

To do this, we will look at the Jewish value of *dorot*, of generations. When we read the Torah, we connect with our earliest ancestors. We connect with Abraham and Sarah, Isaac and Rebecca, Jacob, Rachel, and Leah. We call upon the memory of our ancestors at every prayer service in the *Avot V'imahot*, "*Baruch Atah Adonai, Eloheinu Melech Haolam, Elohei Avraham, Elohei Yitzhak, Elohei Ya'akov, Elohei Sarah,*

Elohei Rivkah, Elohei Rachel, V'elohei Leah—Blessed are You, Adonai, our God, Sovereign of the world, God of Abraham, God of Isaac, God of Jacob, God of Sarah, God of Rebecca, God of Rachel, and God of Leah." We recall our people's deliverance from slavery in Egypt every year at the Passover Seder. We recall loved ones whom we have lost by observing their *yartzeits*, the anniversaries of their deaths. Some commemorate the *yartzeit* of a loved one by lighting a special *yartzeit* candle and/or by reciting the memorial *Kaddish* prayer.

In Judaism, the past is important. The past is important in relationships as well. How you were raised and the kind of marriage your parents have had often plays a major role in how you will behave in your own marital relationship. Similarly, the example you set in your own marriage will influence and instruct others—particularly should you choose and be able to have children (Chapter 5). Even if you do not have children, your relationship will still be an example to family, friends, and community.

Reflecting on the Past

By the time you read this, you have probably had the chance to meet each other's parents several times. However, simply meeting the members of your beloved's family is not enough to uncover the ways in which your partner's past influences his or her understanding of relationships and marriage. In order to truly understand each other, you need to understand what things were like in your homes when you were growing up. But why? Why is what happened so long ago in your partner's life important to you today? After all, we change so much between childhood and adulthood, what possible relevance could the home life of one's youth still have? The answer, it seems, is plenty.

It is in childhood that we learn what marriage is all about. Most of us learn from our parents—whether they are still married or divorced—as well as from other people who surround us.[33] What we see from our parents and others shapes our expectations of what marriage is. "Our beliefs about how husbands and wives should relate, our expectations of rights and responsibilities, our vision of what a marriage should be, lie in our earliest experiences of growing up. How we were cared for, what we witnessed, heard, felt, or imagined about our parents and their marriage formed our fundamental outlook."[34] When we see how our pasts have influenced our understandings of marriage, we can begin to see where our perceptions and expectations agree and differ with those expressed by our partner, and we can begin the conversation of what marriage will mean in this new adventure on which the two of you are embarking.

To begin to reflect on what your home life was like, it might be helpful to engage in the following activity (making an appropriate substitution for "parents" if your family upbringing did not involve two parents, married or divorced):

Exploring Family Love

Many of the ways in which we interact with our partners are shaped by the values, beliefs, and experiences we encountered with our parents, and thus the more we know about our partner's past, the easier it will be to understand some of the conflicts that sometimes emerge. A person, for example, who comes from a family where touch is restricted, may feel quite uncomfortable with a partner who is accustomed to a lot of physical closeness. Others, who grew up in environments where feelings were suppressed, may experience difficulty when expressing themselves to their mates.

For this conversational game, set aside an hour to discuss the following questions of intimacy with your mate. When we listen to such stories of the past, we often feel more compassion toward our partners, and we can better understand the issues they struggled with growing up. Through such conversations, you can begin to transform historical behaviors that may continue to hamper your intimacy and love.

1. How did your parents express their love toward each other, and do you express your love in similar ways?
2. Did you feel adequately loved by your parents, and, if not, what would you have wished them to do?
3. What were your parents' values, and what did they value the most about you?
4. What were your parents' moral and spiritual values, and how are they similar to or different from yours?
5. Did your parents trust and respect each other, and did they trust and respect you? Has your ability to trust and respect others been influenced by your parents?
6. How well did your parents communicate to each other and with you? Do you communicate in similar or different ways?
7. How well did your parents express their feelings of love, sadness, anger, or fear? Were you allowed to express yours, and how did they react when you did?
8. How often did your parents fight, and how did you react when they did? Do you fight in similar or different ways with your

partner and children, or do you suppress the feelings that come up?

9. How did your parents discipline or punish you? Do you think they were fair, and, if not, how do you wish you had been treated? Do you discipline or punish others in similar or different ways?

10. What did you love the most about your mother and your father, and do you find similar qualities in your partner's behavior and beliefs?

11. What did you hate the most about your mother and your father, and do you find similar qualities in your partner's behavior and beliefs?[35]

You probably now have a greater sense of what life at home was like for your partner when he or she was growing up—and perhaps more insight into who your partner is today. As indicated in the introduction to this activity, but worth restating, learning how some of your partner's characteristics have their roots in his or her earliest childhood often makes us more understanding of the differences between us and more aware that, as married partners, we will continue to deal with some things differently.

There is a concept in Jewish law that is relevant to our discussion of the influence of one's family of origin on his or her perception of marriage: *minhag avoteinu torah hee*, the custom of our ancestors is law. Much of Jewish law is based on precedent, interpretation of what the Torah is trying to teach us, the meaning of the laws of the Mishnah, and what the rabbis in the Talmud talked about. This kind of interpretation is the foundation of much of *halacha*—Jewish law—but these sources, revered as they are, do not address all areas of people's experience. Sometimes law is derived from looking at people's behavior. If a custom becomes firmly enough established in a community, it has the potential to become law. Similarly, in our family lives, we do something a certain way not because we know it to be the best way to do something, but because that's the way it was done in our home.

It is easy to think that the way things were done in our homes is the right way of doing them, and that any other way our spouse might have learned and inherited is wrong. We need to remember that our parents' way of doing things is just one way. Our family custom, while important, is not necessarily "right." Our partners had a different way of doing things in their homes of origin about which they may feel just as passionate. The goal is to find a way to talk about your pasts, so that your partner knows why you feel the way you do and to try to find a way to include customs and traditions from both of your families of origin in crafting the way your home and your life together will come to be.

Sometimes these customs that we "inherit" are good things. Perhaps we learned how to be empathic from our parents—or perhaps how to communicate well. These are often the things we like to think about when we think about what we have learned from our parents. But, not all things that we inherit from them are good things. Perhaps we have unresolved hurts from our childhood that lead us occasionally to be insecure or untrusting. Your partner may be able to help you overcome some of your own hurts once the two of you become aware of them. To begin the process of letting your partner in to your resolved and unresolved painful experiences from childhood, it is important to think about what some of those wounds might be and what your partner could do to begin to heal those hurts. The following exercise begins that task:

What I really wanted from my parents was _____

My partner can help me heal this wound by _____

One way in which my mother hurt me deeply was _____

My partner can help me heal this wound by _____

My father once hurt me by _____

My partner can help me heal this wound by _____

The worst thing that happened to me at school was _____

My partner can help me heal this wound by_____

The most painful thing a friend ever did to me was _____

My partner can help me heal this wound by _____

The most painful experience in a love relationship was _____

My partner can help me heal this wound by _____

The one thing from my past I most want to forget is _____

My partner can help me heal this wound by _____

In this relationship, the most painful experience was _____

My partner can help me heal this wound by _____

The things that cause me embarrassment now are _____

My partner can help me heal this wound by _____

The things that cause me shame are _____ _

My partner can help me heal this wound by __ _____[36]

The more you understand your partner, the easier it will be to grow together. It is hard to care for someone when you do not know what he or she needs from you. Participating sincerely in this exercise allows you to learn how to help heal the inevitable—and often invisible—hurts of childhood. The more you understand your partner, the better able you are to see his or her past pain and respond with empathy instead of anger—and the more likely you are to avoid falling into the trap into which some couples fall:

> Partners who married expecting to live happily ever after frequently find themselves in dilemmas that bear some eerie resemblance to one or both spouses' earlier experiences in the family environment. The past—matters that pertain to each mate's own personal history in his or her original family—has a way of surging into the present and becoming a part of the new marital relationship.[37]

It is hard to believe that the past—your partner's childhood—has such an impact on who he or she is today, but time and again, research shows us that one's past profoundly affects who they become. Becoming aware of the impact of *dorot* in your life—that your marriage carries with it the gifts and the baggage of each of your childhoods—will enrich your experience together, and allow you to grow ever stronger in your marriage.

The First Task of Marriage

No matter what your relationship is with your parents, it is going to change with your marriage. It is entirely possible to have a good relationship with your parents and your spouse, but entering into the covenant of marriage with someone must bring about some change. In the second chapter of Genesis (2:24), we find the first statement about marriage and also the first marital advice in the Torah: "Hence a man leaves his father and mother and clings to his wife, so that they become one flesh." This verse suggests that the first step of marriage is to shift our allegiance from our parents to our spouses.

Even though the Torah thinks it important enough to advise the husband (which we would interpret to be both partners) to shift his primary allegiance from his parents to his spouse, this advice was less important in ancient times than it is today:

> [I]n later days the Rabbis fixed the minimum age for marriage at twelve years for girls and thirteen for boys. Under these circumstances it is understandable that the parents took all the decisions when a marriage was being arranged. Neither the girl nor, often, the youth was consulted. Abraham sent his servant to choose a wife for Isaac, and the servant arranged the contract with Rebekah's brother, Laban. Her own consent was asked only afterwards ... When Abraham expelled Hagar from his camp, she took a wife for Ishmael, and Judah arranged the marriage of his first-born. Alternatively, the father might guide his son's choice, as, for example, when Isaac sent Jacob to marry one of his cousins. Hamor asked for Dinah as a wife for his son Shechem, and Samson, when he fell in love with a Philistine woman, asked her parents for her. Even the independent-minded Esau took his father's wishes into account.[38]

In today's world, when people get married as adults, it is important to establish an identity as a couple early on in your relationship. Without your own identity, you will not be able to fully enjoy the benefits of living together as a team.

According to *The Good Marriage*, shifting your allegiance from your parents to your partner is an essential transition for each partner to make. This requires a commitment: "To separate emotionally from the family of one's childhood so as to invest fully in the marriage and, at the same time, to redefine the lines of connection with both families of origin."[39] This means that your partner needs to become your primary confidant. When people tell their parents things that are going on in their lives and don't tell their spouses, it is a sign that there is work to be done. Having your primary loyalty to your spouse also means setting up boundaries with your parents to allow your relationship with your spouse the space it needs to grow. Sometimes that means that your parents need to be less involved in your life than they have been previously, for your primary responsibility is to create an environment in which your marital relationship can succeed.

Jewish tradition reminds us of the sacred relationship between parent and child. The Fifth Commandment instructs, "Honor your father and your mother." Previous *dorot*—generations—have great significance in how you understand relationships. These powerful bonds make it worth restating the main point of this section —while it is important to recognize the role that longstanding relationships have had in shaping your personalities and beliefs, your marriage needs to be your top priority.

An ancient Jewish ritual suggests this first major task of marriage of making your spouse your number one priority quite well. "It was the custom in ancient Judea that a cedar tree was planted when a boy was born and an acacia tree when a girl was born. When they grew up and married, their wedding canopy was made of branches woven from both trees."[40] While before marriage, your identity was represented by the tree that was planted in your honor by your parents when you were born, your marriage marks the creation of something new. This collection of branches marks the blending of your two separate identities into a new relationship; it marks the blending of your two separate pasts—your *dorot*—into a new future.

This custom of the tree planted in honor of a child's birth that forms his or her wedding canopy fits in well with the notion that each of you has three kinds of loyalty: to roots, partner, and covenant.[41] In marriage, a couple still needs to be loyal to its roots. This means that relationships with parents, family, and friends that a person has before marriage are still important (we will pay more attention to this in the next section). But, a second loyalty comes with marriage: loyalty to partner. You have a special relationship with your partner, you support each other, and you love each other in a unique way. Related to partner loyalty is the third kind of loyalty, which again only comes with marriage, the loyalty to covenant. Marriage is more than a contract; it is a covenantal bond. Loyalty to covenant means that the blessing of marriage carries with it a sacred responsibility: to use your love and commitment to make the world a better place. The rest of this section will deal with the issue of loyalty to one's roots—one's *dorot*—by examining the change, including both the challenges and the opportunities, that marriage brings. Later chapters will focus on the issues of loyalty to partner and to covenant.

Changing Relationships with Family and Friends

This change in relationship with your family and friends that comes with marriage can be—and often is—difficult for both you and those you love. When people become more involved with a romantic partner, they typically spend less time with their families and friends. It can be hard for couples to deal with the changes that come in their relationships to friends and family after they get married. Yet these changes are necessary, for any relationship, especially an intimate one, needs space to grow. The need for this space is communicated through *Yichud* (see Chapter 1), allowing a couple a few private moments after their wedding ceremony:

> After the ceremony comes the couple's seclusion behind closed doors, a privilege of marriage. This seclusion, called *Yichud*, recognizes that a marriage whose walls are always open like a *chuppah* is doomed to failure. There must be a time, the bride and groom are told, when they are alone. Indeed, the folk tradition says that there is no greater blessing for new lovers than the wisdom to know when to open their doors and when to close them.[42]

Since you need time to foster your relationship with your partner, you may find that you don't have as much time for family and friends as you may once have had.

Furthermore, as you continue to get to know and trust your partner, you may begin to have him or her fill some of the roles that your friends once did. Your friends may even be jealous of your newly made commitment. Remember that your friends and family love you and care about you—that is what drives their emotions and concern. But you have a job to do. "The task of the first year of marriage is to establish yourselves as a married couple—to become comfortable with your identity as a married pair and adapt to dealing with others as married partners."[43] It is your job to make sure that you are learning how to negotiate life as a couple. This involves setting boundaries as to friends' and family's involvement by ensuring that your relationship has the time and space it needs to flourish.

This is by no means easy! Two Jewish texts show us the conflicting emotions and demands that a new marriage can make on our lives. The first is the oft–cited verse from Genesis 2:24, "Hence a man leaves his father and mother and clings to his wife, so that they become one flesh." On the other hand, we find the saying of Hillel in Pirke Avot 2:4, "Do not separate yourself from the community." Finding a balance between keeping and nurturing important relationships with family and friends and ensuring that your marriage has the time and attention it needs is a challenge, but it is necessary to engage in this struggle to have a deep and meaningful relationship with your partner and continue to foster healthy relationships with other friends and family.

One cannot leave a discussion of relationships with friends and family in marriage without considering how each of you will deal with your partner's *dorot*, those who have helped shape who he/she is today: your in-laws. The next section will turn to that important topic.

In-Laws

We've all heard the stereotypes of bad in-law behavior. These impressions of in-laws have even worked themselves into Jewish humor, playing on the famous story of two women who come before King Solomon each laying claim to the same baby. King Solomon tests the mothers by offering to cut the baby in two and give each woman half. The woman who objects, saying that if that is the solution the other woman should get the baby, is judged by King Solomon to be the real mother since Solomon reasons no mother would allow her baby to be cut into pieces As relates to the topic at hand, it is told this way.

> Early in the last century, there were two young rabbinical students who were matched to be wed to two young women. The two men had never met or seen their prospective brides and had to travel three days by horse and wagon to meet and marry them. Sadly, robbers attacked their wagon along the way, and one of the students was seriously harmed and unable to continue the journey. The one young man who was able to make the trip finally appeared in the city. The two mothers of the brides were quite taken aback when only one gentleman exited the wagon. On hearing the unfortunate story, the two women began to argue, each claiming that their daughter should be the one to wed this healthy young man. As their fight became more pronounced, the townspeople suggested they visit the rabbi of the community to discuss the matter.
>
> After listening carefully to each woman's claim, the rabbi shrugged and said, "Unfortunately, neither of you has a stronger case than the other. I have only one suggestion.

> [As] the wise King Solomon suggested with the baby that two women brought to him, we can cut this boy in half and give each half of him to each of your daughters." Immediately, one woman said that such an idea was preposterous: "Killing the boy would serve no purpose for either of us." At the same time, the other woman strongly agreed with the suggestion: "Yes, what a wonderful idea. Let's rip him in half immediately, and I'm willing to personally participate in the procedure." The wise rabbi stopped both women, stood by the woman who was in favor of his suggestion, and declared, "It's settled then. She's the mother-in-law."[44]

Of course, not all in-laws are like this. Many in-laws do, however, engage in conflict at times. There is no easy answer to in-law conflict. It is important, however, to put it into perspective. Why did this conflict come about in the first place? Often it is because your in-laws get carried away in trying to advocate for what *they* think is best for *their* child. That may be different from what you think—or even what is reasonable—but most in-law behavior, positive and negative, comes out of love for their child, your spouse. Even if the behavior is hurtful, the motive can be noble. Consider the following story:

> Once there was a king who called upon his two soothsayers and prophets to foretell the future. The first came to the king and said, "Your Majesty, as I look into the future, I see a great personal disaster for you and your family. Your two sons will both die before you." The king was outraged at this prophecy and immediately commanded that the insolent soothsayer's head be cut off. Then he called for the second prophet. This time, the wise soothsayer bowed low before the king and said, "Your Royal Highness, I see for you a long and prosperous life. In fact, you are so healthy and virile that you will outlive your entire family." The king was so pleased by this wonderful report that he ordered the prophet rewarded with bags of gold and silver. The moral of the story? It's not the message; it's how you communicate it that counts.[45]

As this story teaches, many in-law problems stem from the way the message is delivered—not from the content of the message. After all, we all want our spouses' parents to care for them. If you stop to consider what the motive is behind a particular issue, you might find that it is just the tone or approach that is bothersome, which is an easier problem to address!

It is true, however, that sometimes in-law relationships can truly be destructive to your relationship with your partner. In rare cases, these relationships can go from the annoying to the abusive. If this is your experience, it is essential to consult with your partner and (hopefully together) confront your in-laws, recognize your commitment to the value of *dorot*, of family, express your love for their child, and address the behavior that is so destructive. If no change results, it is time to talk with someone outside the relationship—whether it is a rabbi or a counselor—who can help you deal with this situation.

To conclude this section, it is only fitting to use words from *The In-Law Survival Manual*, for while we all hope that your relationship with your in-laws will be one that gives you support, comfort, and strength, at the very least it is a relationship that we must survive.

The six letters in the word *relief* represent concept words that are keys to mending and maintaining good in-law relationships. RELIEF stands for:

R Respect
E Engagement
L Loyalty
I Initiative
E Empowerment
F Forgiveness[46]

> *Respect.* As has been mentioned above, try to remember that your in-laws often are looking out for what they believe is best for their child. In addition, it might help to keep in mind that your in-laws are the people who gave birth to and/or raised your partner. That may not lessen the tension, but it might help you understand from where they are coming.
>
> *Engagement.* If you do your best to be in relationship with them, then ideally good things will come out of it. If you give up on the relationship, which sometimes feels like the easier route, then you give up on the potential for growth.

Loyalty. You need to understand that your partner's parents and your partner's past are part of who he or she is. This is what much of this chapter has been about. When you do that, it is easier to accept that your partner's parents are worthy of your loyalty. Additionally, by learning to tolerate—dare we say love?—your in-laws, you show loyalty to your partner by being sensitive to his or her need to have a positive parental relationship.

Initiative. In most in-law relationships, there will be tensions. Left untended, these tensions can erupt into bad conflicts. Take the initiative to deal with problems and discomfort as they arise.

Empowerment. Often, in-law conflicts are over loyalty and control. Allow your in-laws to participate in your lives without compromising in areas that are of particular sensitivity or importance to you.

Forgiveness. In-law relationships can have their rocky moments. While it may well be appropriate to harbor the hurts and disappointments that we may feel towards our in-laws, they can harm our relationships with them in the long run. Being willing and able to forgive goes a long way toward building a strong in-law relationship.

Ideally, this model of *relief* provides comfort as you work on these often tricky—yet vital—relationships with your partner's family, the *dorot* that helped shape the man or woman with whom you're in love!

A Look to the Future

Now that you know your partner's past (and perhaps your own) a little better and on a deeper level, it is important to continue to probe the past and learn what makes your partner who he or she is today. However, it is just as important to look forward to dream of the future that the two of you will create together.

Joseph, our Biblical ancestor, was an interpreter of dreams. While imprisoned in an Egyptian jail, he successfully interprets the dreams of his cellmates—Pharaoh's cupbearer and baker—but the most famous dreams that Joseph interprets are Pharaoh's. Pharaoh has two dreams that that none of his magicians can interpret to his satisfaction and Joseph is summoned by Pharaoh to try his hand. As a result of his prowess in interpreting dreams, Joseph becomes Pharaoh's right-hand man in charge of the distribution of the rations built up during the seven years of plenty when the famine strikes.

Dreams are not just the stuff of ancient history; dreams exist in the modern world as well. Martin Luther King showed us the power of dreams in his "I Have a Dream" speech, given on the steps of the Lincoln Memorial on August 28, 1963, in the midst of the fight for equal rights and equal treatment of blacks in America, particularly in the South. Dr. King concluded his speech by telling his audience—and the whole world- -that he had a dream. "I have a dream that one day this nation will rise up and live out the true meaning of its creed: 'We hold these truths to be self-evident: that all men are created equal.'"

Perhaps we are not as skilled at seeing into the future as Joseph was. Perhaps our dreams do not have the same implications for society as Dr. King's did. Nonetheless, it is important for us to have dreams. Through dreams, we think about what we want the future to look like. The exercises on the next few pages—and in the rest of your married life—afford you have the opportunity to create and share your dreams with each other.

On the next page, you will find a list of categories and questions that can help you begin the process of coming up with your dreams and goals. What is provided is intended to spark your thinking. Feel free to add categories or questions that you feel are important. Follow wherever it leads you. The goal of this is to learn how you want to grow as an individual and as a couple in the near future. Remember that the chapters that follow will help you fill in this list as well, so you may want to come back after finishing your sessions with the rabbi and repeat this exercise.

Over the next weeks, as you talk about your marriage and are given tools to continue to build a strong and happy relationship, begin to think about how you would like your relationship to grow and evolve in the coming years. This is your opportunity to dream. The result of your dreaming can provide guidance in the form of goals that will help shape how you and your relationship develop in the months and years to come. These goals for the growth and development of your relationship are the first step. Once you have some goals to work with, it is time to come up with strategies to help you achieve them. Some tips for goal setting are included below:

- Living the life you envision
- Establish realistic goals in key areas of your life—including personal growth, family, career, spiritual life, and health.
- Discuss your goals and priorities with your spouse.

Beginning to Dream

Intellectual
What do you love learning?
What do you want to do professionally?

_____

Physical
What sorts of physical activity do you enjoy?
How important is physical fitness to you?

_____

Emotional
What makes you feel happy, safe, and comfortable?
What makes you feel sad, lonely, and anxious?

_____

Social
What place should friends (generally) have in your life?
How often do you envision seeing each of your families?

_____

Financial
How do you feel about your current financial status?
What are you saving toward?

_____

Spiritual
What do you enjoy doing?
How do you relax?
How do you want to get involved in the community?

_____

Beginning to Dream

Jewish
What do you do that's Jewish (prayer, Shabbat, holidays, dietary practice,
community involvement) currently?
How do you feel about those activities?
What other activities could deepen the Jewishness of your life?

_____

Personal
What do you feel are your strengths?
What are your weaknesses?
What are you trying to change?

_____

Couple
What do you feel that you and your partner are good at?
What aspects of your relationship are not as you like?
What challenges do you foresee in your relationship?
What values do you want to live out in your relationship?

_____

Family
What influences from your families of origin do you want to replicate in
your marriage? To change?
Do you want to have children? When?

_____

The Larger Community
How could your community become a better place?
How could you be involved to make that happen?

_____

- Keep in mind that a goal must be *meaningful*. Unless you start out feeling that a goal has some [real] value to you, you won't have the drive to spend much time pursuing it.
- A goal must also be *divisible*. In order to follow through on your goals, they must be divided into manageable steps that you can complete on a daily, monthly, and yearly basis. [And, they must be able to be shared between the two of you!]
- A goal must be *tangible*. To realize a goal, you need to have a specific way to measure and observe your progress. If, for example, your goal is to spend more time with your partner, don't just say, "Let's put aside more time to be together." Set up regular date nights for the two of you to do things as a couple—and stick to that commitment.[47]

Making sure your goal is achievable and spending time figuring out how to get there is the first stop on the road to realizing your goal.

It is also important to review your goals on a regular basis to see if you are making progress toward achieving them. If so, keep up the good work! If not, you will need to consider why you are not reaching the goal you set. Is it unrealistic at this point? Is it not as important to you as you once thought? As you and your relationship grow, you will find that things change. What seems important today may seem less so a year or five years from now. Give yourself the flexibility to grow and change by reviewing your goals with your spouse at regular intervals and talking about whether they are still meaningful and appropriate goals for you two to work toward.

Goal setting is an opportunity to begin to think about what kind of home (both physical and emotional) you want your child—or children—to grow up in and work on creating that environment before you introduce children into your relationship and your lives. You can think about how the two of you would like to grow in your relationship to become stronger individuals and a stronger pair. Perhaps one of you wants to be able to express him/herself more to his or her partner. Perhaps one of you wants to become a better listener or better able to respond to your partner's needs and desires. Perhaps one of you wants to become more sexually adventuresome with your partner. Setting goals with your partner helps clue him or her in on what you are working toward so he or she can help you achieve these goals. Goals that you both agree upon then become both of your responsibilities to pursue.

Some of the goals that you two will set individually and together are goals to try to overcome aspects of your family's influence that you don't want to replicate in your own relationship. Perhaps your parents didn't operate on a team model, with both partners having a share in running the household and you think that your relationship should be more equitable in the division of chores. Perhaps your parents had an ineffective way of resolving disputes and you would like to have a more constructive conflict-resolution process. Whatever it may be, it is your opportunity to begin the work of making your relationship into what you want it to become. Through the process of setting goals and dreaming about the future of your relationship, you become aware of your ancestors—your *dorot*—and the influence they have had on you. Through engaging in this process, you not only work to make your relationship better and stronger, you set a solid foundation for the *dorot* that follow you and learn from your example.

Finding Your Place in the Chain of *Dorot*

Each generation learns and benefits from the example of those who came before. It is only because of one generation's bravery that your ancestors arrived on the shores of America.[48] You are the heir of that bravery. This is just one way that a generation is influenced by the one before it. Some of the assumptions you have about marriage and some of the ways you have observed marriage come from your parents. They taught you how to love and be loved (whether their example was positive or negative), they taught you how to communicate with a partner, and they taught you how to (or how not to) organize and divide responsibilities.

An obvious observation works well to sum up this chapter. You are the bridge between what came before you and what comes after you. As you seek to understand life, love, and marriage in your own lives, you will make your relationship healthier and stronger and leave a legacy for the *dorot* that follow you. I look forward to being your companion on that journey!

Chapter 3:
Communication and Conflict
in Intimate Relationships

Everyone agrees that honesty is an important feature in a successful intimate relationship. Not everyone agrees, however, on what it means to be honest with one's partner. Some people, such as psychologist Willard Harley, believe that honesty is defined by full disclosure to your partner, "Reveal to your spouse as much information about yourself as you know—your thoughts, feelings, habits, likes, dislikes, personal history, daily activities, and plans for the future."[49] That's a tall order! We want to be close to our partners, but is it really wise to reveal *all* our thoughts? A Jewish value says that telling the truth to our partners is important. This value is the value of *emet* or truth. It suggests that withholding thoughts and feelings from your partner weakens your relationship.

However, you might wonder, are there ever times that it is okay or even wise to stop short of full and complete disclosure? There is another value that should be considered in setting the framework for your communication as a couple. This is the value of *emunah* or faithfulness—we might also define it as sensitivity. With marriage comes the responsibility to cherish your relationship with your partner above all other relationships. But as this chapter, and your life experience, will make clear, it is not reasonable or appropriate to share all things at all times with your partner; sometimes the relationship is best served by keeping a thought to yourself.

Partners in any intimate relationship must figure out the balance between *emet* and *emunah* to determine what should be shared and what is better left private. To create this balance between *emet* and *emunah* is difficult, but it is perhaps the most important challenge to undertake if you want a successful, lasting relationship. By exploring the basics of successful communication throughout the rest of this chapter, we will begin to see how *emet* and *emunah* interact. For our purposes, we will break down the discussion into six sections: the who, what, where, when, why, and how of communication. We will discuss how to go about ensuring that good lines of communication are open as well as discussing how best to deal with conflict so that your relationship has the best chance to remain healthy.

Who?

Perhaps the most important thing to remember about marital communication is that it involves two separate and distinct individuals who are attempting to relate to each other in a profound way. This tension has been picked up in the titles of two recent bestsellers: *Men are from Mars and Women are from Venus* and *You Just Don't Understand: Women and Men in Conversation*. These titles convey the popular opinion that women and men communicate differently. Whether their premise holds true or not (and we'll explore that a bit below), it suggests that when two people communicate, they come from two different places—in a sense, inhabiting two separate planets. No matter how much time we spend with another person, no matter how much we learn about another person, the other person still experiences life in his or her own way. No matter how long we know someone, we will never be able to accurately guess how he or she will respond to certain things all the time. Rather than being depressed by this thought, see it as an opportunity. The endless quest to know more about our partners, to learn what makes them happy or sad, to learn how they deal with an ever-changing life and an ever-evolving relationship are two of the great benefits of marriage that keep it exciting.

To a certain extent, research supports the view that men and women communicate differently. Studies suggest that men and women react to neutral situations in different ways. Neutral situations are those where neither approval nor disapproval is being communicated. The results may surprise you:

> [M]any wives get into the habit of thinking that if their husbands don't complain about anything, then everything's okay; the wives interpret a lack of hostility as an indication of continued love. In contrast, most husbands seem to think that if their wives don't express obvious affection for them, then everything's not okay; the husbands interpret a lack of overt love as a sign of

37

hostility... This means that men and women tend to differ in their reactions to neutral interactions that are devoid of either affection or animosity: A woman is likely to think things are fine, but a man may start worrying that she doesn't love him anymore. In this manner, gender differences in communication can be problematic.[50]

Of course, these are still generalizations; a given male may not interpret a lack of overt affection as a sign that there is a problem, while a given female might. However, the idea that two people can react to the same circumstances differently is worth noting and exploring and is an argument for *emet* because a dose of truth would erase any doubt about how each partner is feeling.

Understanding that partners in intimate relationships react to the same situation differently means that it is important for each of you to let your partner know your needs. It is impossible for him or her to guess! Of course, this is applicable to any relationship you may have, but it is all the more important to consider and be aware of in this most intimate relationship.

Intimate relationships do not always function in the same way as other relationships. One study found a difference in the type of conflict in friendships and romantic relationships.

Friends were more apt than romantic partners to have mock conflict such as name-calling done for the fun of it. They were also more likely to have nondiscussed and tacit conflicts. Tacit conflicts are those in which the partners discuss the problem in ways that prevent escalation or hurting the other person. Romantic relationships were more commonly characterized by *deja vu* conflicts in which the parties enacted the same conflicts over and over like a broken record.[51]

Understanding the unique nature of communication and conflict in an intimate relationship, we can now probe what each individual in the partnership brings to the interaction. One significant way of accomplishing this is to look, as we did in the previous chapter, at the pattern of one's home of origin. The following questions help prompt reflection on the place of communication, conflict, and resolution in your past and the patterns you might like to continue and those that you and your partner would like to fix:

1. How did your parents express anger? [physically and emotionally]
2. How often did they express anger? Was anyone ever hurt?
3. How would fights start? Who would start them? Who got angry first?
4. How did your parents resolve their conflicts?
5. How did their expression of anger, or lack of expression, make you feel?
6. What did you do when they got angry? How did it affect you, and what did you learn?
7. How did other family members respond to your parents' anger?
8. When you got angry, how were you treated by your parents? Did you feel listened to?
9. Do you currently deal with anger in similar ways?
10. If you have children, do you treat them as your parents treated you?[52]

Remember that knowing about your past helps your partner be more sympathetic to you now. Don't be afraid to reveal your struggles. Focusing on *emet*—truth—will serve you well; it can only help you grow together!

What?

To state the obvious, sharing in an intimate relationship with another requires that each must reveal some of who he or she is to the other person. Not only is this essential for the fostering of a relationship, it also carries emotional benefit. The closeness that results when personal information is shared with another person allows relationship partners to draw ever closer with each other—again an argument for *emet*—for truth in your interactions with your partner.[53]

Perhaps the most important conversation you as a couple can have is a discussion of what each of you is hoping to get out of your marriage. It is not enough to say that you hope that your marriage will make you happy. Successful marriage is first about developing a vision of your future that excites you both, and second, creating an action plan to make it a reality.

A love statement is crafted as a way to express your core values as a couple and take the goals that we discussed in the last chapter to the next level. Once these core values are expressed and written down, they are able to guide you in planning your future. If you engage in this process before your marriage, you will be able to know from your very first day as spouses what you are working toward. A well thought-out love statement also makes an excellent text for the *ketubah*! However, a love statement is not something that can be written quickly, it is the result of a process of thinking, talking, writing, and revising that you and your partner go through to create something that speaks to the totality of your relationship.

Once you have developed a love statement, it is helpful to put it in places that you will look at it often. Some may choose to frame it; others may put a copy in their wallets or their calendars. The important point is that you remember the vision and are able to keep working toward realizing it in your relationship with your spouse. It is also important to review your vision every six months to a year. You and your partner will change and it may be that you want different things out of your relationship than you had wanted previously. Reviewing your love statement allows you to update it for your new dreams and to evaluate your progress toward creating the relationship you want. Creating a love statement requires you to use both *emet* and *emunah*. If you are to create a statement that defines what your relationship stands for and is working toward, it is imperative that it reflect what is important to you, otherwise it will be meaningless. Your love statement must also be built out of *emunah*, a faithfulness that your relationship can continue to grow and improve.

Of course, hammering out a love statement that reflects each of your core values may not be a smooth process since each of you may want different things from your marriage. That's understandable and appropriate, but it can still result in a conflict. Later in this chapter we will discuss how to deal with a conflict, but for now, we need only say that you need not be afraid of conflict. Conflict does not mean that your relationship is in trouble; it simply means that an issue has presented itself that needs both of your attention.

Interestingly, research shows that more often than not, it is the men who are more likely to try to avoid conflict in the relationship. A leading relationship researcher said, "The most important advice I can give to men who want their marriages to work is to try not to avoid conflict."[54] Some issues can only be resolved through conflict. It is important to explore the issue that led to the fight and seek to use it to improve your relationship. Far worse than conflict in an intimate relationship is neglect. Once again we see the importance of *emet*, the open and honest airing of thoughts and feelings, to the functioning of a healthy relationship.

It is easy, in the course of a marriage, to take one's spouse for granted. After all, we think, loving us and caring for us is what our spouse or partner is *supposed* to do. Yet, praising and appreciating one's spouse is essential to marital happiness. According to Michael Kaufman, "It is important that a man should never leave the slightest doubt in his wife about how he feels about her. If there is one attitude in marriage that should never change, it is a husband's expression to his wife of praise and affection."[55] [56] However, our tradition teaches us that praising is not enough. Along with the obligation to praise comes the responsibility to consult with one's spouse. The ancients recognized the importance of this:

> A husband is expected, as an expression of his respect for her, to consult constantly with his wife and to seek her advice and counsel ... [Even if it is not an area that she is particularly knowledgeable about] The Talmud makes this clear [Bava Metzia 59a]. "Even if your wife is short, bend down and whisper to her" [that is, consult with her]."[57]

As alluded to in the introduction to this chapter, however, not all things in a marriage should be discussed. There is a need to balance *emet*, the open and honest sharing of feelings, with *emunah*, the permission for couples to have personal, private space. This is tricky. We live in an age where adultery (which we will discuss in depth later) and addictions are widely prevalent in society. Some might understand the importance of privacy as giving permission to hide such big issues from their spouses. That is not the point! The point of private space is to preserve the individuality of a person who joins with another to form this sacred union. Keeping an occasional thought to oneself is natural and appropriate; keeping a big secret that impacts the health and stability of one's relationship is not.

> Research has also identified that most couples have topics that they have agreed not to discuss. Explicitly or implicitly, partners may agree to steer clear of taboo topics, sensitive matters that, in the opinion of the partners, may threaten the quality of their relationship. Curiously, the most common taboo topic is the state of the relationship itself. In one survey, 68 percent of the respondents acknowledged that the current or future state of their romantic relationships was a subject that was better off not being mentioned.[58]

This is what science is telling us, and it is alarming! It is precisely the issues that we are not discussing that we need to be discussing the most. We need to constantly be looking at our own relationship, checking to see if it is strong, and looking for ways to make it better. We are often afraid to do so, however, because we are afraid of what we will find. Yet by not talking about our relationships, we let problems grow until it gets to be too late and there is no longer anything we can do to fix them. Someone once drew the analogy that a marriage is like a car. A car that is not inspected, that does not have its oil changed, that is not refueled, will soon stop working. A relationship is the same way. Do yourself the favor of a marital checkup to catch and fix problems before they get out of hand; in so doing, you will help yourself find an appropriate balance between *emet* and *emunah*.

Where?

In many ways, this seems to be a silly question to ask. Is there really significance to where a couple communicates? It turns out that yes there is—but for certain issues, it is more important than for others. A discussion of what to have for dinner or which movie to go to see can take place anywhere. In fact, it should happen whenever and wherever you can find a moment. How hard would marital communication be if we always had to find the right place to communicate?

Sometimes, however, we need to have more significant and substantial conversations. Sometimes we need to make significant decisions such as whether or not to take a new job or whether or not to make a big purchase. Other times, we have particular issues or concerns to bring up dealing with the status of the relationship. Still other times, there is a conflict or a difference of opinion to which we are seeking a successful resolution. In these circumstances, it is prudent to be more conscious of the place in which you choose to have these discussions. Interestingly, research shows that such important discussions are best conducted when sitting down or lying down. Standing up causes people to be more aggressive and less patient, both obstacles to effective and productive communication. The only exception to this is if you and your partner find that you can have good conversations and are able to make progress toward resolving issues while sharing in some sort of activity, such as taking a walk, where the other two criteria that will be presented are met.

The next important piece to keep in mind when selecting a place to have an important discussion is finding a place where the two of you can touch. You may choose to talk on the sofa in your apartment or home, or you may choose to go out to a nice restaurant or to a romantic spot to have your conversation, but the ability to touch is important since touch is such a communicator of affection and a hallmark of intimate relationships. "[T]wo people tend to touch each other more as their relationship becomes more intimate. Touch clearly conveys closeness and affection. On the other hand, uninvited touch can be an implicit signal of dominance that establishes one's place in a status hierarchy."[59] Touching *never* means holding a person against their will (this will be discussed more later). Touching is a way of communicating closeness, joint interest, and responsibility for this adventure called marriage—not for intimidation.

The final consideration when choosing where to have important discussions is to select a place where each of you is able to give the other your undivided attention. This means that the TV should be off. If you have children, pick a time when they are out of the room, perhaps out of the house, or when they are asleep. This is because you need to be attuned to what your partner is saying and trying to understand his or her frustrations and concerns, and your partner needs to be doing the same with you.

> Most of us are reasonably skilled and can interpret others' nonverbal messages accurately when we look and listen and put our minds to it. But inattention and laziness can lead us to frustrate our partners by sending mixed messages and misunderstanding their moods and meanings. And there lies an almost certain path to less happiness and relationship satisfaction than we otherwise could have had.[60]

If we have our important conversations where we can give them sufficient attention, then we—and our relationships—benefit.

When?

First, a sobering statistic: "The average couple talks only four minutes per day."[61] Now, the good news. Without drastically changing your lives, you can dramatically increase your communication and greatly improve your relationship. Researcher and relationship expert John Gottman has created a system he calls "The Magic Five Hours." This program is an easy way to set up a habit of communicating at pivotal points during the day and the week.

> **Partings.** Make sure that before you say good-bye in the morning, you've learned about one thing that is happening in your spouse's life that day—from lunch with the boss to a doctor's appointment to a scheduled phone call with an old friend.
> **Time:** 2 minutes a day x 5 working days
> **Total:** 10 minutes

Reunions. Be sure to engage in a stress-reducing conversation at the end of each workday.
Time: 20 minutes a day x 5 working days
Total: 1 hour 40 minutes

Admiration and appreciation. Find some way every day to communicate genuine affection and appreciation toward your spouse.
Time: 5 minutes a day x 7 days
Total: 35 minutes

Affection. Kiss, hold, and touch each other during the time you're together. Make sure to kiss each other before going to sleep. Think of that kiss as a way to let go of any minor irritations that have built up over the day. In other words, lace your kiss with forgiveness and tenderness for your partner.
Time: 5 minutes a day x 7 days
Total: 35 minutes

Weekly date. This can be a relaxing, low-pressure way to stay connected. Ask each other questions [that help you get to know your partner better.] (Of course, you can also use these dates to work out a marital issue or work through an argument you had that week, if necessary.) Think of questions to ask your spouse (like "Are you still thinking about redecorating the bedroom?" "Where should we take our next vacation?" or "How are you feeling about your boss these days?").
Time: 2 hours once a week
Total: 2 hours
Grand Total: Five hours![62]

It might seem forced to plan out these moments. Wouldn't it be better if we were able to be a bit more spontaneous? Perhaps yes, but it is worth getting into the routine of taking advantage of the time that Gottman suggests simply because it has been proven to be so beneficial. And if you've gotten good at "The Magic Five Hours," don't stop there! Any time you add beyond the five hours above will strengthen your relationship further.

We need not buy into the specifics of Gottman's plan. His point, however, is clear—if we wait for the perfect moment, we'll miss out on dozens of opportunities to connect. Over the course of a week, the little moments are easy to skip because they seem so small, but they add up to a substantial amount of time. So use Gottman's suggestions or find your own pockets of time; just make sure that you and your partner keep connected to one another!

Why?

This section will make the case for good communication between spouses, for the benefits of this communication are many. Simply stated, learning effective communication tools now can influence how happy your marriage is likely to be as time goes on. "The more unexpressed irritants participants have in their relationships, and the more they report minimizing or avoiding the discussion of conflicts, the less satisfied they are."[63] Open and honest communication (*emet*) really is a pathway to a happier and healthier marriage!

Jewish tradition recognized that learning to communicate well was of great importance. "To have a good marriage, husband and wife need to feel that they can talk to each other with perfect confidence in each other's discretion. Solomon declares [Proverbs 18:21]: 'Life and death are in the [power] of the tongue.'"[64] Communicating well gives life to your relationship because it allows you to grow stronger as a couple.

Fostering good communication between spouses is a sign that the two partners have a good grip on reality. Some enter marriage with the idea that they will never quarrel. Unless one partner is subsumed by the other and never expresses his or her wishes or individuality, the two of you will have times when your opinions and desires clash. Movies and storybooks tell us that it's possible to live happily ever after. Yet, learning how to communicate well prepares you for the reality of marriage where "two people in love and happily married, will have misunderstandings, will occasionally fight, may hurt each other's feelings, and will have periods of boredom and frustration."[65]

There is nothing abnormal or wrong in a couple having conflict; in fact, there are many things right with it. So, when you have your first married fight, even if it is on your honeymoon, do not think that you have just made a big mistake. Use it as an opportunity to practice your communication skills and to celebrate the two distinct personalities that have decided to share a life together!

There is a real benefit to fostering good communication skills and using them with your partner whenever the two of you have a deep conversation or conflict. Fights resolved with respect, compassion, and love can strengthen the bond that a couple shares, for "the understanding and compassion fostered by good dialogue reduces the You vs. Me attitude that stands in the way of intimacy, and replaces it with a renewed sense of *We*."[66] A good relationship is based on a team model. Conflicts provide the opportunity for your team to grow stronger through tackling a problem together and working out a solution together.

How?

We've spent a lot of time talking about the basics of good communication without describing how to do it. Now it's time to roll up our sleeves and look at some models of effective communication in the hopes that you can find one that works for you or find different pieces that work together. Finding a model of good communication is too important to risk trying to fit every couple into one model. Learning how to communicate effectively is not easy, and many authors recognize this. An example is Michael Kaufman who uses a Biblical story to illustrate his point: "The Torah relates that Jacob toiled for Rachel for fourteen years in order to marry her. But when he stood under the marriage canopy with her, his real work had only begun."[67] This suggests that no matter how hard we have worked to get to this point; the road ahead is more challenging (and also filled with the potential to be much more rewarding!).

Communication Techniques

Communication is a complicated process that can take many different forms, some productive and some much less so. Mark Goulston and Philip Goldberg suggest four levels of communication and four levels of listening. The four styles of communication deal with how one partner talks to the other. Goulston and Goldberg describe this by using four "D" words, arranged from least to most productive:

> Diatribe—talking *over* each other.
> Debate—talking *at* each other (with no one really listening).
> Discussion—talking *to* each other in a calm, pleasant manner.
> Dialogue—talking *with* each other.[68]

Most productive conversation takes place at the dialogue and discussion levels. The same is true with Goulston and Goldberg's listening levels, this time all beginning with the letter "R," each level representing a higher level of respect:

> With *removed* listening, the person is in the room but not really present.
>
> *Reactive* listeners hear what you say, but take issue with everything—often in a combative or condescending manner.
>
> *Responsive* listeners hear you out and respond appropriately and respectfully to the content.
>
> With *receptive* listeners, direct eye contact and the absence of fidgeting, interruptions, and other signs of impatience extend a genuine welcome mat.[69]

Again it is the last two styles, responsive and receptive listening, that yield the best results. Reflect on your conversations and figure out at which level they are most often located. If you often find yourself in the debate or diatribe mode when talking or in the removed or reactive mode when listening, you have found an area that needs significant attention in your relationship!

The rest of this section will give you techniques to communicate in the more desirable half of Goulston and Goldberg's four categories. Some basic principles can guide you in creating clear and good communication.

One writer offers us this piece of wisdom:

> I *think* about what I say *before* I say it.
> I *listen* to what I say *as* I say it.
> And I *reflect* upon what I say *after* I say it.[70]

Another popular marriage guide offers a more extensive list:

Ten Steps to Clear Communication
1. Figure out what you want to say. Before you talk with your spouse about something, make sure you know what you want to tell him or her to minimize potential misunderstandings.
2. Decide what you need from your spouse. You are more likely to get your needs met, whether it is a hug or an answer to a question, if you know what you want.

3. Use good judgment in timing. Is your spouse sick or preparing for a big meeting at work? Consider your partner's state of mind when choosing a time to talk.
4. Make eye contact. Your spouse will be more likely to listen and hear you if you are looking right at each other.
5. Get your spouse's undivided attention. You will not be heard if your spouse is thinking about something else when you are trying to talk with him or her.
6. Be a good listener. By being attentive to your spouse, you will have a more productive discussion.
7. Confirm that you were heard. Ask your spouse if he or she fully understands what you just said. Then, and only then, will your spouse be able to respond properly.
8. After your spouse has told you something, rephrase what he or she has said. This will let your spouse know for sure that you've heard what he or she is saying.
9. Schedule a better discussion time if necessary. Sometimes it's just not possible to get your spouse's attention at the exact moment you want it.
10. Remember that communication is a two-way street.[71]

The short-term goal of good communication is to identify and resolve conflict. The long-term goal is to allow couples to grow closer together, to replace that sense of "You vs. Me" with a sense of "We." The two of you are on the same team. If you remember that, it will be easy to treat your spouse with the compassion and sensitivity due your life's partner.

Just as there are several things *to* do in order to have effective and meaningful communication with your partner, there are also things *not* to do. John Gottman suggests that in order to have a productive conversation, one should stick with the issues and respect our partners and not fall into the following bad habits that lead to frustration and/or miscommunication:

1. Kitchen-sinking—combining every frustration into a fight triggered by a particular incident.
2. Off-beam conversations—conversations which drift off topic instead of addressing the issue that triggered the conflict.
3. Relying on mindreading—one partner *assumes* he or she understands the other partner's thoughts without checking those assumptions with the partner.
4. Interrupting—not letting one's partner finish his or her thoughts.

5. Yes-butting—constantly finding fault in one's partner's suggestions.
6. Cross-complaining—responding to a complaint or criticism that one partner makes with a complaint in return instead of tackling the issue.[72]

Each of these bad habits hinders our efforts for constructive communication. They are so dangerous because these habits are so easy to fall into. It takes a team effort to ensure that it doesn't happen. Each of you needs to be watching for signs that your communication is drifting away from the one-issue, respectful conversation model that Gottman presents and to attempt to regain control of the conversation to ensure that it is as productive as possible!

Gottman makes another observation that seems self-evident, but research shows that it is a significant cause of strife in our intimate relationships. Simply put, we treat our spouses differently than we treat our other social relationships. It is not uncommon in intimate relationships for partners to forget to say please and thank you to each other or not to be particularly respectful of the other, when we would never dream of speaking to our friends in this manner! Words of wisdom from Jewish tradition sum up a key lesson. Ecclesiastes 9:17 tells us "Words of the wise are spoken pleasantly."[73]

This is the ideal in terms of our communication with our spouse, but sometimes anger is unavoidable. A great Jewish scholar of eight hundred years ago, Asher ben Yehiel, said, "Do not be angry with your wife; if you push her away from you with your left hand, do not delay to bring her close with your right hand." At first it may seem that Asher ben Yehiel is suggesting that we never be angry with our partners. The second part of the text however reveals his point. Anger is a human emotion. It is important that the relationship be a safe place for the expression of anger—a place where people need not be ashamed of their feelings and emotions, nor stifle them. Yet couples must be careful that anger not erode the essential foundation of *emunah*, faith, that both partners are committed to building a meaningful and fulfilling marriage.

Conflict Resolution

It would seem, given the extraordinary divorce rate nowadays, that we are communicating less well with our partners than previous generations did. We can indict television, computers, and increased travel with making communication more difficult than it once was. I believe, however, that technology and increased mobility is only part of what is going on. In modern times, husbands and wives are called on to communicate about things that previous generations never discussed. Previous generations did not have to decide who does which chores in the same way that we do now (an issue that will be discussed in greater detail in Chapter 5). It was assumed that the wife would take care of the house while the husband went to work. In previous generations, the man was the head of the house and made all the "important" decisions about what the family would do—when they would be able to go on vacation, when they would move, when they would be able to buy a new appliance. Modern couples working on the partnership model need to decide all these things together, providing fertile ground for disagreements to arise. Therefore, it is more important than ever that couples learn how to communicate effectively.

Of course, good communication is not a cure-all. It is only natural that two people whose lives are so intertwined will occasionally have conflicts with each other. Models of negotiation in business have some applicability to marriage. One of the key texts in the business world is called *Getting to Yes*. It is a manual for negotiating the difficult terrain of interpersonal relationships. From this classic book, William Betcher and Robbie Macauley have distilled some principles that apply quite well to marital communication and negotiation:

1. Separate the personalities from the problem. Attack the second, not the first.
2. Focus on interests, those on both sides, not predetermined positions.
3. Invent some options that permit both to gain, which means find a way of making the pie bigger before you divide it.
4. Concentrate on keeping the process of negotiation fair rather than debating details of substance. If you reach agreement on a fair way to divide the pie, no one can then complain about getting the smaller piece.[74]

Betcher and Macauley remind us that it is very easy to take the opportunity of a quarrel to bring up those things about your partner that you don't like and wish would change, but using the occasion of a quarrel to bring up this kind of issue is counterproductive; Gottman labeled it "kitchen-sinking." The other valuable insight from this model is that we should focus on a person's reason for taking a particular position. Once you see that there is a reason, a want, or a desire behind a particular position, you will almost always find that there is an agreeable solution that meets many of your mutual needs—if not everything that you ask for.

According to *Close Companions*, this is not what most couples are doing today. Most couples are engaged in "conflict-avoiding" marriages, when the healthiest relationships are "conflict-resolving" marriages. Here is how they describe the differences between the two types.

> *The Conflict-avoiding Marriage.* This is an apt description of the average couple of today. The culture tells them very plainly that people who really love each other don't get into conflict, which of course is not at all true. When in fact they do develop serious disagreements, they have no appropriate skills to deal with the situation. After a few bitter quarrels, one or both may be so deeply hurt that peace at any price may seem the best deal to make. The only way to do this is to withdraw from each other. Physical withdrawal is of course not usually practicable; but psychological withdrawal is. The usual procedure is to close off areas of the relationship that prove to be explosive and to choke back intense feelings that might start a fight. In this way the couple make their life together tolerable by limiting their areas of interaction to those that can be safely handled. This of course means settling for a superficial relationship and giving up all hope of loving intimacy. People who do this find themselves denied the warm and tender love they hoped to find in marriage. Such people easily become disillusioned and are ready to turn elsewhere for the meaningful relationship they failed to find. Among these are the unhappy, frustrated husbands and wives who are divorcing in large numbers today.
>
> *The Conflict-resolving Marriage.* This is simply another way of describing the enriched marriage. As I have already said, conflict is not something tragic in a human relationship. It is not to be feared and run away from. It is a normal and integral part of any close relationship. It is in fact raw material to be worked on and transmuted into an opportunity to grow. A conflict may even be welcomed because it pinpoints an area where an adjustment has to be made—very much as an unusual noise in an automobile engine locates a fault, which, when corrected, makes

51

the machine run more smoothly. Couples who learn the necessary skills to work on their conflicts therefore have the assurance that they are continually improving their relationships. Each conflict resolved marks another milestone in their progress toward relationship-in-depth.[75]

This highlights the important notion that conflict is a natural part of intimate human relationships. Marriages seek to combine two distinct people into a unit. These two people have differences and sometimes those differences come into conflict. What is important is that we not be afraid of conflict, not be afraid of expressing our true thoughts, *emet*, to our partners, but that we balance it with the sensitivity for our partner's feelings and respect our partner's dignity, as the value of *emunah* suggests. Rather, we should accept our conflicts and allow the differences that conflict highlights to enrich the marriage, not threaten it.

Kaufman summarizes the main points of the conflict-resolving marriage:

One of the hallmarks of a good marital relationship is not constant agreement, or the absence of disagreement, but rather the ability to calmly discuss and work out disagreements in ways that are reasonably satisfactory to both parties. The way to avoid quarrels is to discuss difficulties and problems freely and openly and try to work them out. This is the best way to stop anger and resentment from building up. The Sages urge couples to make every effort to ensure, when they tackle a problem, that an exchange of views does not deteriorate into an angry quarrel. Husband and wife should practice the art of peaceful, calm discussion—allowing the other to have his say, responding calmly, and avoiding angry, abusive tones.[76]

Once a conflict starts, there are many ways of defusing it. Often, however, we fail to seize these opportunities to begin to repair the ill will engendered by a fight. Emotions often run so high that we pass right by opportunities to defuse the conflict. John Gottman suggests that people, in the course of a fight, will make what he calls "repair attempts." These repair attempts are things we might say or do that suggest that we would like to get off the highway, to deescalate the situation. A list of repair attempts follows on the next page. One of the best things you can do for your marriage is to learn how to use and how to spot repair attempts. It will save you many hours of heartache and allow you to discuss the many important issues that a quarrel raises.

Ideally, in time, each conflict finds a successful solution. But David Mace, one of the great premarital counseling experts of the previous generation, says that a successful resolution of a quarrel should not be the end of the issue. Perhaps more valuable than finding a resolution to the issue causing the dispute is going back over the quarrel and learning from it. Mace puts it this way:

> Nothing I can offer you will help you more than to learn the habit of examining your negative feelings to each other. Use your quarrels to practice this art. Go back over what happened, share with each other how you felt, discover the root of the difference between you, and find a way of digging it out. Do this over and over again in every negative exchange in which you become involved. Turn all your negative interactions into positive interactions. If you can do this, with or without counseling help, the goal of a mutually satisfying relationship is within your reach.[77]

To conclude this section, let us turn to Jewish tradition. The Torah (Exodus 34:6) instructs that God is "compassionate and gracious, slow to anger, abounding in kindness and faithfulness." As creatures created in the image of God, I hope that we can bring these same sensitivities to our human relationships—especially into marriage.

Children and Conflict

There is some disagreement among counselors as to what degree children should be privy to the fights and quarrels of their parents. I side with those who suggest that it is not a bad thing for parents to quarrel in front of their children—provided that they make up in front of their children as well. Part of the negative stigma attached to fights is that they too often happen in secret. If children see that fights can occur in a loving and committed relationship, they will be less fearful of fights in their own intimate relationships. If they feel that fights are something to be hidden away, something secret, then they will be secretive about their fights and squabbles in the future. Once we allow children to see our quarrels and

Repair Attempts

Often, using these phrases—or phrases similar to these—is an attempt by one of the partners in the relationship to deescalate the conflict. When the other partner is sensitive to this effort by his or her mate, progress can be made toward ending the conflict.

I feel
1. I'm getting scared.
2. Please say that more gently.
3. That hurt my feelings.
4. I'm feeling sad.
5. I feel blamed.
6. I'm feeling unappreciated.
7. I feel defensive.
8. I don't feel like you understand me right now.
9. I'm getting worried.

Getting to Yes
1. You're starting to convince me.
2. I agree with part of what you're saying.
3. Let's compromise here.
4. Let's find our common ground.
5. I never thought of things that way.
6. I think your point of view makes sense.
7. Let's agree to include both our views in a solution.
8. I see what you're talking about.

I Need to Calm Down
1. Can you make things safer for me?
2. I need things to be calmer right now.
3. Just listen to me right now and try to understand.
4. Tell me you love me.
5. Please be gentler with me.
6. Please help me calm down.
7. Please be quiet and listen to me.
8. This is important to me. Please listen.
9. I need to finish what I was saying.

Adapted From John M. Gottman, Ph.D. and Nan Silver, *The Seven Principles for Making Marriage Work* (New York: Crown Publishers, Inc., 1999) 173–5.

Repair Attempts

Practice using and listening for these phrases in your conflicts and see if they help propel you toward a resolution! Some people choose to put this sheet in a prominent place (like in the bedroom or on the refrigerator) in their home so they can refer to these when the need arises.

Stop Action!
1. I might be wrong here.
2. Please, let's stop for a while.
3. Let's take a break.
4. I'm feeling flooded.
5. Please stop.
6. Let's agree to disagree here.
7. Let's start all over again.
8. Hang in there. Don't withdraw.
9. We are getting off track.

Sorry
1. My reactions were too extreme. Sorry.
2. I want to be gentler to you right now, and I don't know how.
3. Tell me what you hear me saying.
4. I can see my part in all this.
5. How can I make things better?
6. Let's try that over again.
7. What you are saying is …
8. Let me start again in a softer way.
9. I'm sorry. Please forgive me.

I Appreciate
1. I know this isn't your fault.
2. My part of this problem is …
3. I see your point.
4. Thank you for …
5. That's a good point.
6. We are both saying …
7. I love you.
8. One thing I admire about you is …
9. This is not your problem—it's *ours*.

conflicts, however, it is vitally important that children see that fights get resolved, so if you fight in front of your children, don't be afraid to make up in front of them either!

A Word about Violence and Abuse

Violence has no place in a marriage, yet it happens with alarming frequency. Two sobering statistics alert us to just how big an issue domestic violence is. A 1989 FBI study concluded that in the US a woman is battered at least once every fifteen seconds. Another study estimated that violence will occur at least once in two-thirds of all marriages.[78] And lest you think that this is not a problem that affects the Jewish community, research shows that the incidence of abuse in the Jewish community is comparable to levels within the general population.[79] It is impossible to have the kind of marriage that this book encourages you to foster when one partner abuses the other. I urge you, whether you are the partner who is abusing your spouse or if you are the one being abused, *get help!* Find someone you trust to help you at this most difficult time—whether it is a counselor, a clergyperson, or a help hotline. No marriage can—or should—long survive the physical and emotional pain that violence introduces.

Wrapping It Up

A major theme in this chapter has been the tension between *emet*, or truth, and *emunah*, or faithfulness. We see time and again the importance of letting our spouses into our world. We want (and need, if we are to foster a healthy relationship) our spouses to know us well. It is crucial that we reveal ourselves to them and that we listen to what they would like to share with us.

It is just as important that we think about how we talk with our partners. We owe them respect; they have chosen to share life's journey with us. We owe them politeness—just because we share the same home and bed does not mean that we can take our spouses for granted. In order to have a loving relationship, we must do our best to remember that how we say things can matter as much or more than whether we say them at all.

This is the dialogue between *emet* and *emunah*. There are many ways to tell the truth. We should seek out the most loving and compassionate way to share our concerns and our frustrations with our partners. This is the secret of good communication.

Chapter 4:
Investing in Your Marriage

If you had to guess right now what this chapter will be about, what would you guess? Some will see the word investing and immediately assume that this chapter is about money matters. After all, you're getting married and your financial picture will, at least in some ways, change. Others may look at this and be expecting a chapter about the effort required to maintain a healthy relationship. Both would be right. In researching happy and healthy marriages, I have come to believe that important lessons about maintaining a healthy marriage can be gleaned from a financial model and vice versa, that important lessons about finances can be learned from understanding how emotional ties are fostered and strengthened.

To best get at these comparisons, I would like to share an idea that some psychologists and students of the human condition call the "Emotional Bank Account." We are all familiar with a financial bank account. All of us have them. Our bank accounts allow us to deposit money and withdraw it to pay bills. Most will not be familiar with the idea of an emotional bank account, however. Willard Harley defines the concept for us: "Within each of us is a Love Bank that keeps track of the way people treat us. Everyone we know has an account and the things they do either deposit or withdraw love units from their accounts. It's the way your emotions encourage you to be with those who make you happy. When you associate someone with good feelings, deposits are made into that person's account in your Love Bank."[80] This is to say that a nice thing that someone does for us or a time when that person meets our expectations makes a deposit in our love bank account for that person. We are going to focus in this chapter on the most important account in your love bank: your spouse's.

The good news is that as most couples approach marriage, their love bank accounts are in decent shape—if they were not, they would be delaying the marriage or breaking off the relationship. But a healthy emotional bank account at the time of marriage does not determine that there will be a healthy account a month, a year, or a decade from now. But don't think for a moment that there is nothing you can do to keep a positive balance in your emotional bank account! This chapter will be devoted to giving you the tools to keep a healthy balance in both of your bank accounts—emotional and financial.

To do this, we will look at the emotional and financial bank accounts from three different perspectives. First, we will look at the immediate future and seek to figure out how to keep a positive balance on a day-to-day basis. Next, we will look at the short-term picture, which will largely focus on developing a cushion in these accounts so that when bad times come, we have enough emotional and financial strength to weather them. Finally, we will focus on the long-term—looking ahead to ensure that the groundwork is laid for a stable financial and emotional future.

However, before diving in, it is important to pause and introduce this chapter's guiding value: *acharayut* or responsibility. We all want to have money in our bank accounts and a surplus of goodwill in our emotional bank accounts. The responsibility for ensuring that that happens lies with both people in the relationship. To succeed in marriage financially and emotionally requires the full and complete participation of both partners. As Rabbi Tarfon says in Pirke Avot 2:16, "It is not up to you to complete the task, but neither are you free to desist from it." If we interpret that "task" that Rabbi Tarfon wrote of as building a successful marriage, then this brief quote teaches us several important lessons.

1. Your participation is a necessary part of the effort to build a happy and healthy relationship, for you are not free to desist from working on your relationship with your partner.
2. You and your partner need to work together to create the kind of marriage you want, for one person cannot complete the task alone.
3. Creating a positive marriage requires both partners to feel a sense of responsibility, *acharayut*, for the future of your relationship.

Rabbi Tarfon does not suggest that this task is easy—for it is not. He does, however, remind us how important it is that we work with our partners to build the best and strongest marriage we possibly can!

Day-to-Day Living

There are certain financial and emotional tasks that must be done on a regular basis in order for a relationship to succeed. On the financial side of the coin, the basic responsibilities sound simple, but many couples find meeting them on a regular basis to be difficult and stressful. For some, marriage marks the first time that they are responsible for managing their finances. Others have lived alone for a period of time and were responsible for themselves, but now they are entering a partnership arrangement with another person. Still others have considerable experience with financial management, but are learning how to manage money with a new person who has his or her own expectations.

Your Views of Money

As with so many things in life, there are few hard and fast rules about money management. Much of it is dependent upon the two of you setting parameters for how you will treat money in your relationship. Here is where the idea of *acharayut* comes into play. It is easy to ignore financial issues because people are often so divergent in their attitudes about money that money becomes a stressful subject that arouses strong feelings—or there is stress because a couple is anxious about whether they will have enough money to pay their bills, take a vacation, or any other thing that they might want or need to do. The conversation about your views of money that this chapter encourages —and revisiting it every so often—will strengthen your relationship. It is the responsibility of both partners to make your perspective on money known and to participate in crafting a financial plan for the two of you that merges both of your understandings of the use of money. To do this, you need to take time to learn about your own perspective on money and that of your partner. To introduce this conversation about how you and your spouse view money, take a moment to consider the following two quotations:

> If a man is so fortunate as to have found a good wife, he shall never miss anything. Though he may be poor, he may regard himself as rich. For, as the Bible intimates (Proverbs 31:10), it is easier to obtain precious stones than to find a good wife. Where there is love and trust between husband and wife, there will be riches and contentment; but if they hate each other, the contrary must happen. They shall miss everything if their hearts are divided (Hosea 10:2).[81]

On the other hand:

> These days, when everyone is concerned with earning a livelihood, a person should prepare his house first and his income, and only afterwards should he take a wife.[82]

Both quotes use the male-gendered language that was more typical when they were written—try to get beyond that. Read these quotations as applying to both genders, consider the following questions, and then share your responses with your partner.

- Does one text speak to you more than another?
- Do you see parts of both that you like?
- Do you believe, as the first text, that love conquers all?
- Do the above texts suggest different kinds of wealth?
- If yes, which is more important to you?

This activity provides an introductory hint as to your attitude about the importance of financial stability and security in your life. Keep your responses and use them to sharpen your understanding of your view of money, what it is used for, and how it should be managed, and to allow you to understand your partner's views of money, where they are similar to yours, and ways in which they may be different.

To begin to understand how you view money, it is important to examine several questions. The following questions serve as an introduction for this inquiry:

- How much money do you need to feel secure?
- How often do you worry about money, and why?
- How has money caused problems in previous relationships?
- In your relationship, who directs or controls the money, and how does it [the control] make you feel?
- How do you feel about your partner's debt, income, and savings? Your own?
- How does it feel to make less (or more) money than your partner?
- Do you deal with money differently than your partner, and do you have different values?
- How have money issues interfered in your present relationship?

- What do you think your partner's greatest difficulty with money is?
- What is your greatest difficulty with money?[83]

If you are honest in completing this activity, you may begin to see patterns that allow you to understand your own relationship with money and the similarities and differences between your view of money and your partner's. (Remember that differences do not mean that there is a weakness in your relationship. Differences—once one is aware of them and able to deal with them—can strengthen your relationship as your perspectives can help balance each other.)

The following short exercise asks you to make two marks and your partner to make two marks. Each of you should make a mark for how you see yourself falling on this continuum and each of you should make a mark as to how you see your partner.

Spender————————— —————————————————Saver

The spender often thinks that money is designed to be a source of enjoyment. On the other hand, for the saver, money is often a source of security. When a spender and a saver marry, the two styles will often come into conflict. It is near impossible to change someone. The best course of action, therefore, is to learn to live with and to recognize the value of your differences. For example, if one of you is a spender and the other a saver, the spender can strive to see the benefit in working toward having enough money for a trip, or even thinking as far ahead as retirement, perhaps seeing that saving money can provide security. The saver can see the benefit in living life more in the here-and-now that the spender offers, perhaps finding that a different attitude toward money has aspects that are freeing.

If the two of you have similar styles, then you need to work together to make sure that you don't go too far in the direction of your shared tendency—if you are both spenders, it is important to make sure that you don't spend beyond your means; if you are both savers, it is important that you remember to have fun and treat yourselves every now and again.

Responsibility for Money Matters

As a couple, you have many decisions to make. One of the most important issues to discuss is how to handle money within your marriage. The amount of money you have is less relevant to marital happiness than how you manage that money. Fortunately, there are many different options from which you may choose. There are four main systems of family money management according to the British sociologist Jan Pahl:

> The "whole wage" system in which one partner (usually the wife) manages all household finances; the "allowance" system in which the husband divides responsibility by giving the wife a certain amount for household expenses but keeps control over the rest; the "shared management" system in which partners have equal access to and responsibility for all family money; and the "independent management" system in which each partner manages a separate income exclusively.[84]

This quotation gives four examples, but by using your creativity to respond to your needs and strengths, you can find ways to combine these different options and even perhaps create new ones.

Long before Pahl identified these four kinds of money management, Jewish scholars and sages considered the financial relationship of a married couple. "The Sages advise that a married couple's possessions should be jointly owned, and bank accounts jointly controlled. A man's relationship with his wife is governed by the principle, incorporated into Jewish law, of *ishto k'gufo,* she is like his own body."[85] This conclusion would seem to suggest that only one of the four options presented by Pahl is correct.

Jewish tradition, however, does not deem wrong the other three options of money management as a couple. The key concern of the sages is mutuality and equality. It is important that both partners be equally invested in the relationship if it is to be meaningful and fulfilling. If both names are on the checks and both are equally responsible for the financial health of the family, the sages reason, then both are equally committed to the relationship. Of course, sharing control over the finances does not necessarily imply a commitment to a shared destiny, just as choosing a different style of money management does not mean that the commitment to a shared destiny is absent.

Once again, it is the value of *acharayut* that should be your ultimate guide in figuring out how to manage money within your relationship. It is the responsibility of both partners to come up with a system that allows you the control you want over your finances.

Income vs. Expenses

Your short-term financial success is realized when income and assets exceed expenses and debts. This means that you are able to pay your bills and still have money left in the bank. To do this, you must do careful budgeting. It is important to look at all the places from which you get income and all of the things that you spend money on in a given month and make sure that you're aware of and comfortable with the difference between the two. Perhaps you make far more than you spend and can afford a better lifestyle than you realized. Perhaps you make far less than you spend and you need either to take on debt or find ways to cut items out of your expenses to even out the two sides of the equation.

There are many ways to accomplish this task. One way is to record all money you make and all places you spend money for a couple of months. What you will have at the end of this period is an initial glimpse of how you are doing on the income-expense balance sheet. It will help to put expenses in categories and make sure that you are comfortable with what you are spending in each particular category each month. If not, you have the opportunity to change where you spend your money in the future and to change the balance between income and expenses. A helpful way of doing this is to identify expenses that are fixed or essential, such as food, rent, electricity, and medical insurance. Most of the time when you are looking to rein in your spending to bring it more in line with your income, the adjustments to your spending must come from items that are more discretionary, such as buying a daily cup of coffee, going to movies, or eating out. If cutting those discretionary expenses still does not yield enough savings, it might be time to discuss ways to trim even within the "essential" expenses. You could move to a smaller apartment or house and pay less in rent, you could buy less expensive food at the grocery store or shop at a less expensive market, or you could become more conscious of your use of power—remembering to turn off the lights when you leave a room, turning up the air conditioning a few degrees in the summer, and turning the heat down in the winter.

Another option is to use financial management software. There are several programs on the market that help you to look at your overall financial position and help you to create a budget to stick to and the tools to help monitor your progress. The convenience of computers and the ability of financial management software to organize and analyze financial records make these programs a good investment for many. In fact, many banks and credit cards are compatible with these programs, allowing transactions to be downloaded directly into the software, minimizing the manual recordkeeping you need to do.

A third option for creating a budget is to see a financial planner. It can be very helpful to talk over your financial issues with someone outside your relationship who can look over your financial picture without the emotion that you and your spouse bring to money issues and help you get your spending and saving into an appropriate balance.

Computer programs and time with a financial planner cost money. It is easy to think that since you are trying to save money, you don't need either of these aids. Getting a handle on your income and expenses is so important, however, that the money invested in setting up a workable pattern will pay off down the road.

This discussion, once again, suggests that the core value at work here is *acharayut*—that the two of you have the responsibility to work on a financial plan that allows you to cover your basic expenses with the income that you have.

Before leaving this discussion, it is important to spend a moment talking about *tzedakah*. *Tzedakah* is defined as the charitable contribution that is incumbent upon every Jew. According to Jewish tradition, *tzedakah* is not an option; in fact, even one who receives assistance from *tzedakah* funds must give *tzedakah* (Gittin 7b). As you work on your budget, remember to figure an amount to give to *tzedakah*. Perhaps you want to settle on a percent of your annual income. Perhaps you want to figure out an amount to give at the beginning, middle, or end of each year. Once you have money that you can give to charitable causes set aside, you and your partner can decide where it goes. Perhaps there is a cause about which one or both of you is passionate. Perhaps you each decide where half of the money goes. Giving to *tzedakah* is another important way that you show *acharayut* with your financial management—showing a responsibility to the needs of the community and a commitment to important causes working to make the world a better place.

Keeping a Positive Balance in the Emotional Bank Account

At the beginning of this chapter, I introduced the idea of an emotional bank account. This account works in a similar way to a bank account, in that it is possible to make deposits and take withdrawals. The great difference between an emotional bank account and a financial one is that the emotional bank account is kept inside each of us, instead of at a bank where our finances are stored. Since we don't get a statement from the bank every month indicating what our balance is, tending to the emotional bank account takes a different kind of accounting. Before we get there, however, it is important to figure out what types of things constitute deposits and withdrawals in the emotional bank account. "When our most important emotional needs are met, the largest of all Love Bank deposits are made."[86]

What, then, are our most basic emotional needs? There are many wants and needs at our emotional cores. What follows is a list of just a few that are important to most people. At the bottom are some blank spaces for you to add some of your own key emotional needs.

- To feel loved
- To feel that you can trust
- To feel valued
- To feel important
- To feel respected
- To feel intelligent
- To feel talented
- To feel attractive to your spouse
- _____
- _____

Making deposits in the emotional bank account is in some ways easier than making deposits in the financial one. To make a deposit in your emotional bank account, you don't need to go to work—you don't even need to have a job. You do, however, need to listen to your partner, respond to your partner's expression of need, and value your partner.

One way of figuring out what the core issues are for you—and what will result in the largest emotional bank account deposits—is by probing what intimacy means to you. To help facilitate that reflection, here are some questions for you to ask each other:

- What does intimacy mean to you?
- What form of intimacy do you desire from me?
- What kind of intimate exchange would you like in the morning, the evening, and the afternoon?
- What would be your fantasy of the ideal intimate weekend?
- What fears or problems have you had, or do you now have, with intimacy?[87]

Share your answers with your partner, allowing him or her to know what emotional needs are most important to you and, just as importantly, to get to know you better.

By learning what is important to your partner, you become what John Gottman calls an emotionally intelligent person. When both of you are aware of the other's emotional needs, including your partner's definition of intimacy and what your partner's hopes and dreams are, then you become an emotionally intelligent couple. This emotional connection is very powerful and profound.

The key is to be in tune with your partner. This takes time and effort, and it requires responsibility or *acharayut*. Both partners need to be responsible for trying to learn about the other's emotional world and doing the best they can to respond to what they learn. This will surely result in deposits into the emotional bank account!

Sometimes, however, we make withdrawals from this emotional bank account. We are all human and sometimes we can be insensitive or forgetful and sometimes our actions (or inactions) get misinterpreted by our partners, and they lead to a withdrawal. If the marriage is a priority, however, the deposits should outweigh the withdrawals. That does not mean that withdrawals can or should be ignored; it is important to repair the damage done by any emotional withdrawals that might be taken. We make deposits when we apologize sincerely for what we've done, by growing from the mistake that led to the withdrawal in the first place, by doing nice and thoughtful things for our partners, and in countless other ways that we show our partner that he or she is important to us and cherished. It is each partner's responsibility to ensure that a healthy positive balance remains in the emotional love bank.

The Short-Term

Now we know about the day-to-day system of deposits and withdrawals from financial and emotional bank accounts. However, that is not the end of what is important to learn about and to consider. In both bank accounts, it is important to have a short-term plan. As before, we will consider the financial first.

Planning Beyond Today: Finances for the Short-Term

We've discussed deposits and withdrawals and budgeting. Yet, the budgeting we've discussed so far only deals with managing from paycheck to paycheck. Every couple needs a financial plan that looks into the future because we do not know what life has in store for us. So, how do we plan for the unknown? We plan by recognizing and preparing for certain possibilities. That does not mean that we will be fully prepared for anything and everything that happens in our lives, but it does increase our chances of being able to weather life's inevitable storms. What happens if the car needs a repair, if one of you loses a job, if one of you gets sick? None of these are pleasant things to think about, but they are real.

The easiest way to prepare for life's unpredictability is to save some money (perhaps three to six months' salary) in an account to which you have easy access. This means that you should keep this money in a savings account or some other place where there is neither a heavy penalty nor a significant delay should you need the money immediately.

A further investment in preparing yourself against life's unknowns is insurance. There are many different kinds of insurance related to protecting you against a short-term (or long-term) crisis. Below is an outline of some of the major kinds of insurance. You and your partner should talk with an insurance agent (or several) and decide what kinds of insurance it makes sense for you to get at this point in your life.

- **Auto Insurance**—Required in most states in order to drive. Covers your car in the event of accident and pays for damage you cause to another car. Most auto insurance also covers you for a certain amount of personal liability, covering medical expenses for injuries resulting from the accident, up to a certain limit.

- **Property Insurance**—If your home or apartment is burglarized or (with some policies) damaged by fire or earthquake, your insurance will reimburse you the amount that you have lost, up to your insured limit.

- **Medical Insurance**—Covers you in the event of illness or hospitalization. All different kinds of programs exist with all different kinds of costs and benefits. Talk with your partner and a reputable professional to make sure that your medical coverage is adequate.

- **Life Insurance**—In the event that you or your spouse should die, life insurance provides the surviving partner with money. Many people purchase life insurance when they have children so that their offspring would be provided for in the event that one or both parents should die.

- **Disability Insurance**—Covers you in the event that you are unable to work. Both short-term and long-term disability insurance policies are offered. Most disability insurance policies have a set time before they kick in, so it is still important to bank several months' salary even if you purchase disability insurance.

I am not suggesting that all of this insurance is necessary for every couple. It is important that you figure out, however, what insurance you want to have and that you allow for payment of the insurance premium in your budget planning. Again we come to the realization that this discussion is all about *acharayut*, responsibility. It is your responsibility to make sure that your checkbook balances in the present—and that you have planned for some of the challenges that life might bring.

Allowing Your Relationship to Grow

Just as it is not enough for a couple to focus only on the present of their financial picture, so too it is not enough just to focus on the emotional present without being concerned about the future of your emotional bank account. The theory behind this section is similar to the previous section. You want to have enough emotional deposits to weather difficult times. For example, if one of you is seriously ill or is suffering from a bout of depression, you want to have built up enough goodwill and love to allow you to be patient with each other when times are tough. Banking emotional deposits when you're feeling well allows you and your partner to go through the bad times and still have a surplus in your emotional bank account.

There are several ways to make emotional deposits for the future of your relationship. One thing to do is post the list on pages 70-71 in a place where you and your partner will see it often. Every week—and optimally on the same day every week—you and your partner should select an item from that list. You need not both select the same item, but both partners should initial the task they select. By the end of the year you will have tried every item on the list once. This activity makes additional deposits in the emotional bank account because each of them is an emotional gift to your partner. It is a gift of kindness, support, and love that can only serve to strengthen your relationship. You may find that some tasks are easier to accomplish than others are, but you should challenge yourself to try each one on the list. Also, do not worry if you aren't perfect at your chosen task—just the effort involved will show your partner that you're committed to improving your relationship. Pirke Avot 2:16, which was referenced earlier in this chapter, teaches that "it is not your responsibility to complete the work, but neither are you free to exempt yourself from it." Engaging sincerely in the process of keeping your relationship fresh and continually working on making it better is what Jewish tradition challenges us to do. We are not asked to be perfect—just to work to make our relationship as strong and fulfilling as it can be!

Another way of making large emotional deposits is to engage in fun, spontaneous activities together. It is the memory of these surprises or fun times that can sustain you in more difficult times that inevitably come in life. Here is one list of spontaneous activities to try:

- Do something unpredictable and creative.
- Avoid ruts. Use your imagination.
- Go to an amusement park without your kids.
- Take a day off from work and spend the day together.
- Remember that "because it's fun" is a good reason to do something.
- Finger paint.
- Get messy.
- Have a pillow fight.
- Dance. If you can't get to a club, turn on the stereo and boogie in the living room.
- Take adult education classes together.
- Learn a foreign language.
- Play sports, but don't keep score.
- Paint a mural on a wall.
- Go hiking or biking.
- Clean the house together. Yes, this can be fun too!
- Go ice skating in the summer and swimming in the winter.
- Build sand castles at a local beach.
- Do a jigsaw puzzle together.
- Go to a comedy club.
- Go to the zoo.
- Lighten up.[88]

When you do these together, you feel good. You build up a store of good memories that can only increase the balance in your emotional bank account!

52 Ways to Work on Your Marriage

___ ___ 1. Do something novel for your partner

___ ___ 2. Be courteous to your partner

___ ___ 3. Don't belittle your partner

___ ___ 4. Make sure your partner is number one

___ ___ 5. Call your partner by his or her pet name

___ ___ 6. Praise your partner in public

___ ___ 7. Resolve today's problems today

___ ___ 8. Be flexible

___ ___ 9. Plan ahead for a special dinner/getaway/event

___ ___ 10. Avoid bringing up sensitive issues for your partner

___ ___ 11. Look nice at home

___ ___ 12. Be reliable

___ ___ 13. Don't promise more than you can produce

___ ___ 14. Admit your own shortcomings

___ ___ 15. Be appreciative

___ ___ 16. Give extra attention to your family

___ ___ 17. Don't expect your partner to be what he/she is not

___ ___ 18. Keep yourself interesting

___ ___ 19. Pay extra attention to your sex life

___ ___ 20. Be tolerant of your partner's interests and recreation

___ ___ 21. Do not permit yourself to be unhappy in your job

___ ___ 22. Eat healthy and exercise

___ ___ 23. Don't nag

___ ___ 24. Don't criticize your partner's family

___ ___ 25. Add a little spice and surprise to your life

___ ___ 26. Tell your partner you love him or her frequently

Excerpted from Michael C. Venditti, M.D., *How to Be Your Own Marriage Counselor* (New York: The Continuum Publishing Company, 1980) 191–232.

52 Ways to Work on Your Marriage

__ __ 27. Keep your bad moods to yourself

__ __ 28. Be optimistic about your partner's motivations

__ __ 29. Do something together that your partner likes doing

__ __ 30. Don't compare your partner with anyone else

__ __ 31. Don't criticize your partner

__ __ 32. Acknowledge your partner's efforts and improvements

__ __ 33. Don't hold a grudge

__ __ 34. Go to bed at the same time

__ __ 35. Share your successes and glories with your partner

__ __ 36. Give 90 percent in hopes of getting 10 percent in return

__ __ 37. Keep some fun and good humor in your marriage

__ __ 38. Admit your mistakes and apologize for them

__ __ 39. Reevaluate your marriage and plan improvements

__ __ 40. Try to eliminate the traits your partner finds irritating

__ __ 41. Pay attention to your spiritual life

__ __ 42. Have a date night

__ __ 43. Look through a photo album together

__ __ 44. Do a chore you wouldn't ordinarily do

__ __ 45. Notice the things your partner does right

__ __ 46. _____

__ __ 47. _____

__ __ 48. _____

__ __ 49. _____

__ __ 50. _____

__ __ 51. _____

__ __ 52. _____

*Note: There are spaces next to each of these ideas for you and your partner to check off. Also note that forty-five suggestions are given. The last seven are for you and your partner to determine and to write in.

The Sentence-Completion Game

Ask your partner to pick a topic: it could be money, sex, childhood memories, politics, feelings, vulnerabilities, anger, self-image, God—wherever your imagination wants to go. Using that topic as a focus, you then create a partial sentence—a sentence stem—that your partner is to complete. For example, you might say, "The thing I like most about money is _____." Your partner then says the first thing that comes to mind—*as fast as he or she possibly can*—without censoring of worrying about the result. It doesn't even matter if the sentence makes logical sense.

After your partner has responded, you create another sentence stem, or repeat the same one again. If you do use the same sentence stem, your partner must say something new. By asking the same question three or four times, you can guide your mate deeper into his or her self. Give your partner about ten or twelve sentence stems and then switch roles, having your partner make up stems based upon the topic you first chose. Then pick a new topic and play a second round.

This game provides an excellent way to explore sensitive relational issues, but almost any topic you choose will uncover aspects about your partner's personality and preferences that you had not known about before.

The following examples of sentence stems will help to get you started, but the real fun comes when you can create new ones as you go along. Feel free to ask about the past *("As a child, I dreamed about _____."),* to speculate about the future *("When I'm ninety years old, I want to _____."),* or explore a wild fantasy or fear.

- My most important quality is _____
- If I allowed people to really see me, _____
- My deepest fears are _____
- My deepest longings are _____
- My favorite way of being touched is _____
- When I look into your eyes, _____
- The strangest thought I've ever had is _____
- The most difficult issue I face in marriage is

    _____
- If I could have one fantasy come true, it would be

    _____
- Life seems most fulfilling when _____
- Life seems most painful when _____ [89]

When you know your partner better, you know better how to relate to each other, you know better how to make your relationship stronger and healthier and how to best reflect the love and commitment you have toward each other.

Additionally, it makes your partner feel special and valued when you let them know they're cared for.

> It's so important to make each day count with your spouse. Most people let days, weeks, or even months go by without letting their partner know how important he or she is to them. That won't happen to you if you make a point of doing one nice thing a day for your spouse. Whether it's something small, such as preparing a special meal, or something large, such as planning a surprise vacation together, you will be acknowledging the importance of your relationship on a regular basis. Even a small thing as calling from work and saying, "I love you," can make his or her day special.[90]

So we see that "small" things really aren't that small after all!

Once again, the responsibility—the *acharayut*—to strengthen your relationship in good times to provide cushion in tougher times and to make your love stronger every day lies in both of your hands. Take advantage of the opportunity of sharing life with someone to get to know your partner and to find happiness in making your partner happy. That is one of the greatest things you can do to create a marriage that is wonderful and fulfilling.

The Long-Term

When you get married, you are making a commitment to your beloved to be his or her partner for life. In addition to the day-to-day living that you must figure out and planning for the short-term, it is important to also think about, plan, and prepare for a time many years down the road.

Financial Planning for the Long-Term

You might say, "We're just getting married and starting our lives together— how long-term do we really need to look?" The answer is that by planning now for the future—even thinking as far ahead as retirement—you can greatly impact the money you have available at the time you choose to retire because the money you deposit today earns interest and will be worth far more when you want it at your retirement. For example, say you are able to invest $1,000 per year in an account that has an interest rate of 5 percent. In 20 years, having put in $20,000, your account will be worth $34,719.25—73 percent more money than had you just put it under your mattress! If you have an account with a greater average interest rate, you'll wind up with still more money. Also, should you choose to have children, it can only help you to think about saving for their education since college costs continue to rise at a rapid pace.

Some companies offer retirement benefits, perhaps making contributions to your pension plan or matching whatever contributions you make into your own plan. Others do not, but you can always set up a retirement account—an IRA—on your own through the bank. If you can make contributions and still meet your obligations for the immediate term and the short-term as outlined above, then making contributions to a retirement account will help provide financial security later in life.

Most retirement accounts work by allowing contributions but not allowing withdrawals (at least without a significant penalty) until a specified age. Talk with your partner about beginning to make contributions toward your retirement and come up with a plan for the immediate moment. Review your retirement plans periodically, perhaps every year, and see if you can contribute more into your account and if there are any other plans you want to begin. The goal is that when you want to retire, your financial situation will allow you to do so. Getting to that point requires starting to think about and plan for retirement early and taking responsibility for the discipline required to plan now for something so distant.

Emotional Bank Account: Long-Term

To begin to understand the importance of emotional intimacy to the long-term happiness in your relationship, it helps to understand the transformation that happens for most couples over the course of their relationships:

> Robert Sternberg ... proposed that three different building blocks combine to form different types of love. The first component of love is *intimacy*. It includes the feelings of warmth, understanding, communication, support, and sharing that often characterize loving relationships. The second component is *passion,* which is characterized by physical arousal and desire. Passion often takes the form

of sexual longing, but any strong emotional need that is satisfied by one's partner fits this category. The final ingredient of love is *commitment,* which includes the decisions to devote oneself to a relationship and to work to maintain it. Commitment is mainly cognitive in nature, whereas intimacy is emotional and passion is a motive, or drive. The "heat" in a loving relationship is assumed to come from passion, and the warmth from intimacy; in contrast, commitment reflects a decision that may not be emotional or temperamental at all ...

When hundreds of couples who had been married at least fifteen years were asked why their marriages had lasted, they *didn't* say that they'd do anything for their spouses or be miserable without them, like romantic lovers do... Instead, for both men and women, the two most frequent reasons were (1) "My spouse is my best friend," and (2) "I like my spouse as a person." Long-lasting marriages seem to include a lot of companionate love.

[W]e can conclude that there appear to be two major types of love that frequently occur in American marriages: a love that's full of passion that leads people to marry, and a love that's full of friendship that underlies marriages that last.[91]

Research shows that a couple's friendship is what sustains them in later years and the emotional investments that this chapter has been talking about have provided some tools for maintaining and enhancing that friendship.

Jewish tradition, although not bashful about the place of passion in a marriage (as we will see in the next chapter), also recognized that the key to a long-term successful relationship is in building and nurturing a friendship. "The years of romance and intense sexual activity are shorter and less enduring than the years of sustained, lifelong friendship."[92] Even Maimonides (Rambam) commented on this almost a thousand years ago in his commentary to Pirke Avot 1:16. His statements on friendship are summarized by Rabbi Shlomo Aviner:

Romantic love between a husband and wife certainly has its place, but it is not the main essence. Much, much deeper is the Rambam's classification of three different types of affinity and friendship:

Friendship that gives pleasure:
We enjoy each other's company; it feels good to be together.

Friendship that provides security:
I trust you and can depend on you. I'm not alone; I have someone to tell my secrets to. I have a good friend with whom I get along very well.

Value-oriented friendship:
We both want to reach the same goal and we help each other along the way.[93]

It is each partner's responsibility, knowing how relationships and marriages tend to evolve over time, to lay the groundwork for a strong friendship with a strong emotional connection and commitment to each other. It takes work, but it allows the two of you to develop a stronger connection with each other and allows your love to grow in significant and powerful ways.

Conclusion

Creating a good marriage is a huge responsibility, but one that brings with it tremendous rewards. We focused in this chapter on the financial and emotional bank accounts, and how to maintain them on a day-to-day basis, in the short-term, and over the long-term. According to Kaufman, "[M]arriage must be based primarily on knowledge of one another and on mutual giving."[94] In being givers—of our attention and ourselves to marriage—deep, lasting love takes root and grows.

Chapter 5:
Building a Fulfilling and
Successful Home Life

Most will be familiar enough with *The Wizard of Oz* to recognize Dorothy's famous declaration, "Toto, I have a feeling we're not in Kansas anymore!" Dorothy was on a mission in a strange place with strange yet loveable companions. She yearned for the comfortable and the familiar. In a word, Dorothy dreamed of home. For her, going back to the security and comfort of home was as simple as clicking her heels together and saying "There's no place like home."

For those who prefer sports to *The Wizard of Oz*, think about a baseball game. The batter stands at a place called "home." Once he leaves, his goal is to get back to home. On the base path, he is subject to being picked off, thrown out, or caught in a rundown. Once the runner is home again, he is safe.

Just as home is important to Dorothy and baseball players, so too has it been important to Jews throughout Jewish history. When the Israelites arrived and settled in the land of Israel some three thousand years ago, they were finally able to build a permanent Temple to God. During all the years of wandering in the desert, the Jews had used a portable ark, but now, settled in the Promised Land, they could establish a permanent place to worship God. King Solomon, David's son, was elected to build this glorious Temple. For such a great site, one so important to Jewish tradition, we would imagine that a unique word would be used so as not to confuse this holy place with anything else. Yet, that is not what happens. This great structure is called a *bayit*, a home. It is a home for the Israelites and for God. It is a place where the relationship between the Israelites and God reaches its deepest and most profound level. As the locus for the people's encounter with God, the Temple occupied the center of the Jewish people's religious life.

The Temple is not the only place where *bayit* appears in the Jewish lexicon. It is important to note that *bayit* often appears as *beit*. It means the same thing even though the words sound different. Three words using the word *beit* (*bayit*) will shed light on the meaning of this word.

> ***Beit K'nesset***—literally "a house of assembly," but commonly translated as synagogue.
> ***Beit Sefer***—literally "a house of the book," but commonly translated as school.
> ***Beit Tefilah***—literally "a house of prayer," but commonly translated as sanctuary.

We see from the presence of the word "house" in all of these words that the house is an important concept in Jewish tradition.

The word *bayit* also forms the foundation for an important Jewish value, *sh'lom bayit,* or a peaceful home. We should strive to create an atmosphere of peace in our homes. This is perhaps what underlies Rabbi Jose's statement, "I have never called my wife 'my wife,' but I called her 'my home.'"[95] A home that brings this kind of comfort is not easily built, however. It is the result of lots of hard work, but the results are tremendous:

> The Jewish home is called a *mikdash m'at,* a Temple in miniature ... According to Judaism, when there is *sh'lom bayit* in the home and love between husband and wife, they have created a miniature and holy Temple.[96]

This chapter begins the conversation on several topics that greatly affect the happiness and stability of the home that you two are about to create together. May the foundation that this chapter provides help you build a strong and healthy home together.

Chores

It might seem strange that household chores even make the list of important things to discuss in order to have a successful marriage, yet here they are. The division of housework is, in actuality, a critical step in the creation of a happy home.

When a couple agrees upon an equitable division of chores, their relationship is enriched. This is a relatively new idea—things used to be a lot different in American marriages. The home used to be almost exclusively the sphere of the woman and the workplace the sphere of the man. It was the man's job to bring home the money and it was the woman's job to keep the home in order.

> If the husband could keep his household under control, and could get his wife pregnant at regular intervals, those were all the skills that he needed. And if the wife could cook, sew, keep the home reasonably organized, be sexually available to her husband, and take adequate care of her children, she could measure up satisfactorily to what was expected of her.[97]

Today, many marriages operate on a different model. Often, both partners work. It is no longer practical, nor desirable, in many marriages for the wife to be the one solely responsible for the home. This has led to a drastic shift in the way many modern couples run their homes.

Based on the principle that the one who controls the resources has the power, it was usually the working spouse, most often the male, who had the power in the relationship. In many respects this was easier—*not* better.

> When husband and wife had their own spheres to govern, there was greater harmony because there was far less opportunity for dissension. Granted, the modern way is more considerate and more democratic, but it is not smoother. Nothing runs more smoothly than an absolute dictatorship.[98]

This suggests that, in determining how to take care of our homes, we are more likely than generations past to have disagreements and quarrels. Given this observation, we would do well to remember that conflict is not necessarily bad. Because marriage involves the meshing of two individuals into one marriage, there is likely to be conflict from time to time. We also remember that it is nothing to be afraid of, but something that requires attention and patience to work out.

The concept of separate spheres introduced in the last quotation is also important. In the typical relationship of the past, the spheres of husband and wife had very little overlap. They inhabited the same house, but the husband typically had little responsibility for its care. Today's model of a companionate marriage (as discussed in Chapter 4) is different:

> A companionate marriage is founded on the couple's shared belief that men and women are equal partners in all spheres of life and that their roles, including those of marriage, are completely interchangeable. Both husband and wife lead important parts of their lives outside the home. While one partner, usually the wife, may take time out from her career to devote attention to young children, she remains committed to both work and family.[99]

When both partners have significant parts of their lives outside the home, both must work together to take care of things within the home.

When the division of chores becomes a topic of discussion within a marriage, it becomes clearer that household chores are a way of strengthening your marriage—not just mundane things that must be done in order to allow your marriage to exist. When all—or most—of the household chores were one person's responsibility, it was pretty easy to make sure that they got done. In our more egalitarian society, how exactly do you go about splitting up chores equitably? There is no one right answer—it is up to each couple to decide what works best for them. Perhaps it works best for you to take turns doing the laundry, or perhaps one of you is quicker at folding than the other so you agree that one of you will throw the laundry in and the other will fold it. Or perhaps it makes sense for one person to have laundry as his or her job and the other partner takes care of taking out the garbage and cleaning the bathrooms.

Other couples devote time when they will both be home to taking care of the chores. So while one is doing the laundry, the other takes out the garbage and cleans up the dishes. This model works best when the specific chores are laid out in advance so that it is clear what chores you are hoping to accomplish.

Some people suggest listing all of the chores that need to be done, their frequency, and amount of time they usually take. Once all that information is listed, it is possible to come up with an appropriate and balanced division of chores. This kind of list also allows you to divide chores based on strengths. If one of you is handy and the other is all thumbs, it would make sense for the one of you who is handy to do the chores that involve fixing things. The other partner, then, would be able to do another chore. If one of you can't stand dusting and the other doesn't mind so much, then it only makes sense for the one who doesn't mind dusting to do it.

Other couples come up with different models for accomplishing household chores. How you go about dividing them isn't important. What is important is that the division be equitable and that both partners feel that the other one is contributing appropriately to the completion of household chores.

Establishing a way of dividing chores is not something that should be taken lightly. Research shows that a feeling of equity in the area of household chores is a key component of a happy marriage—as important as an equitable division of responsibilities for childcare.[100]

Equity does not mean equal, however. Say, for example that one of you works ten-hour days and the other works six-hour days. The one who works the shorter days has more time at home and may reasonably be expected to take care of more of the household tasks. However, just because one person works shorter hours does not mean that he or she must take care of all of the tasks. It is important that both partners feel that each is contributing to the maintenance of the home you share.

Chores are the tools that allow you to build the home that you want. They are a way that you make a daily statement that this relationship is important to you. Chores are holy too. In the ancient *bayit*, one of the jobs given to the priests, those who offered the people's sacrifices to God, was to take out the garbage. Without that task being performed, the whole system would not have worked. If you learn to think of chores as opportunities to welcome holiness and closeness into your relationship, and to demonstrate your commitment to your partner, they might not seem quite so arduous!

Sexual Intimacy

What a difference fifty years can make! Fifty years ago, couples who lived together before marriage were "living in sin." Now many couples choose to live together before they get married. Fifty years ago, premarital sex was a rarity, now it is common. I do not by any means intend to pass judgment on whether couples should or should not live together and/or engage in premarital sex, only to reflect the reality of the contemporary world. These changes mean that the conversations that a rabbi needs to have with a couple about sex in marriage are almost completely different from what a rabbi would talk about with a couple fifty years ago.

In addition, there is so much more expression of sex in our culture and society. What is seen and talked about in television shows and movies today would have been unimaginable in public places fifty years ago. Scores of magazines line the bookshelves offering sex advice. With so much information out there, what is left to talk about? Plenty. Movies, television shows, and magazines can give a dangerously inaccurate picture of sex in marriage that can harm this important aspect of your relationship together and impact the relationship as a whole.

This section will not utilize many statistics such as how many times the average couple engages in sexual intercourse because, in reality, comparing yourself to those numbers has no bearing on your own sexual satisfaction. Should you want to see statistics, they are readily available in books, magazines, and on the Internet to those who are curious. This section is about a way for you, as a couple, to create a sexual relationship that is pleasing and fulfilling for the two of you.

A myth exists that shows how things have changed in the last fifty years: "Years ago, people married so they could have sex, but today many people feel that by marrying they are *giving up* their sexual freedom."[101] This is a prevalent myth, but as this chapter will teach, it need not be the case.

Good Sex

It is a common belief that the more often couples have sex, the better their relationship is. For some, this is the only measure of satisfaction with their sexual relationship. This perception is not entirely untrue, "What distinguishes those people who have fulfilling sexual relationships from those who don't? You might guess that people who have sex more often are happier with their sex lives, and in general, you'd be right."[102] Yet this is not a complete, nor even the primary measure that we should use in determining sexual happiness. The real key to happiness is how close the relationship is between desired and actual frequency of intercourse. "People who stated that their actual frequency of sexual intercourse was very close to the level of sexual activity they preferred were more likely to report that they were happy in their marriages."[103]

This is why statistics are irrelevant or even harmful to your sexual relationship. It is not the frequency as compared to the national average that matters; the key to satisfaction with your sexual relationship is whether your particular sexual needs and those of your partner are met. "It will help married couples to remember that they are not involved in sexual competition, in aiming at a world's record for quantity or quality of orgasms. They are in bed because they love their mates, love each other both physically and spiritually."[104] Some men have high sex drives, others are happy with an occasional sexual experience with their partner and the same is true with women.

Some guidelines can be offered to shape how you and your partner develop an understanding of what is good sex for you,

[H]aving frequent sex is not necessarily the same thing as having good sex. Having good sex would seem to depend on:

- Each person having his or her needs met by a partner who respects the other's specific sexual desires.
- Having the proper balance of positive and negative interactions (sexual and nonsexual) in the relationship, so that there are more positives than negatives.
- Enjoying being with each other, in bed and out of it.[105]

The most important thing is that you learn what is important to your partner and work to make sure that your sexual needs and those of your partner are met. A good sexual relationship is no more complicated than that!

Ethical Sex

"Uh oh," you might be saying. "Here's where the rabbi lectures us on appropriate sexual behavior—all the things that Jewish religion says we can't or shouldn't do. I don't want to sit through a discussion of all these prohibitions." Jewish tradition is actually very permissive when it comes to a couple's sexual relationship. "All forms of sex play between husband and wife are considered legitimate and are permitted as long as the aim is a greater natural fulfillment. The ideal is that the sex act be not perfunctory and dutiful, but that the experience be as exciting and fresh as the first union on the wedding night (Rabbi Meir in Niddah 31b)."[106] The key here is that Jewish tradition teaches that if *both* partners are comfortable, then it is a perfectly appropriate thing to do. We will talk about extramarital relationships later, but another source highlights the Jewish view of sex between married partners:

> The Jewish ideal of holiness is achieved both by renunciation of the illicit and the sanctification of the licit. One becomes holy not merely by avoiding forbidden sexual relations, but also by *participating in sanctioned marital relations,* and by doing so in a decidedly human way. Thus, sanctification means performing the act as a *mitzvah,* in fulfillment of a command of God, with a

measure of restraint and sensitivity for one's partner, and
with *kavanah,* proper intent.[107]

This is quite a progressive outlook on sex and sexuality—particularly
for texts written over a thousand years ago. It means that you have the
permission of the Jewish religion to experiment with your partner to find out
what is sexually fulfilling to both of you. "Judaism looks upon intercourse
in marriage, not as something sinful, not as a regrettable necessity, but as a
beautifully meaningful experience which enhances the love of husband and
wife. Every form of sex play which leads to that end was approved."[108]

Some have taken the meaning of sexual intercourse to a deeper level
still, attaching cosmic significance to sex between two married partners.
Maimonides wrote, "When a man and his wife unite sexually in holiness,
the *Shechinah* [presence of God] rests between them."[109] Sex is so powerful
that it can bring the presence of God down to dwell among humans. Sex
also reveals the unity of the two distinct people in the marriage:

According to Jewish tradition, there are two distinct purposes for
sex:

> The creation stories in the Torah suggest two purposes of
> sexual activity. The first and most obvious is *procreation.*
> Sex is part of God's plan for populating the world; it fulfills
> God's will for both animals and humans. The rabbis used
> the words of Isaiah as a proof text: "The creator of heaven
> who alone is God who formed the earth and made it,
> who alone established it. He did not create it a waste, but
> formed it for habitation."

> The second purpose of sexual relations is *companionship,*
> which the Torah seems to regard as an even greater
> justification for sexual relations than procreation. In
> Jewish tradition, the belief that "it is not good for man to
> be alone" is as important if not more important than the
> command to "be fruitful and increase." The Torah uses the
> term *yada*—to know—to indicate a sexual relationship.
> Sex is thus considered more than a mere biological act;
> it involves intimate knowledge shared by two human
> beings.[110]

In modern times, it is no longer taken for granted that a couple will want
to—or be able to—have children. This topic will be taken up in greater

length in a later section. What is important to note is that Judaism recognizes and celebrates a purpose for sex beyond procreation. Sex as companionship is an important value held in Jewish tradition, and it is yet another gift that a healthy sex life gives to you as a couple.

A Voice from Tradition

One reason that people give for cheating on their partners is that loving the same person had gotten stale and they needed a change. An ancient Jewish ritual long observed by traditional women is being adapted by some liberal couples to keep their relationship perpetually fresh. This ritual is called *nidda*. In its traditional context, it arose because the blood of a woman's menstrual period was frightening and largely misunderstood. It was thought best to stay away from her during this time, called the time of her "impurity." As a result, from the onset of a woman's period, she would be separate from her husband for the duration of her period (generally five to seven days) and another week after that. At the end of that time, she would go to the *mikvah* (Jewish ritual bath) and cleanse herself. She and her husband could then have sex for the remainder of the month.

Now we know more of what happens when a woman has her period. It is less frightening to us. Some have however reclaimed the *nidda* ritual as a way of keeping the sexual relationship fresh and exciting. This understanding of *nidda* is not new:

> According to our sages, it is natural for married love to have its ups and downs: R. Meir used to say, "Why did the Torah command a *nidda* to abstain from marital relations? [Because] if the couple becomes too familiar with each other, their union loses its attraction. Therefore the Torah prohibits her to him ... so that on the day of her purification she is as attractive to him as she was on their wedding day." In other words, maintaining a state of constant burning desire is untenable. [Nidda 31b][111]

The separation and coming together that the *nidda* ritual introduces elevates sexual intercourse from something mundane to something truly holy. "In Judaism, not having sex whenever one desires with whomever one desires, but limiting it instead to certain times and certain contexts, makes sexual intercourse a holy act."[112] A further benefit offered by Jewish tradition for this practice of *nidda* is that in this period of sexual separation from each other, the couple is free to focus on other aspects of their relationship. "The required abstention from marital relations, and all intimacies that may lead to them, for twelve to fourteen days each month, can be explained as providing a medium through which Jewish couples can develop a strong, healthy relationship rooted in a mutual attachment other than that of a sexual bond."[113] As with other elements of Jewish tradition, you are encouraged to try this practice to see if it adds to your experience of marriage or not. Some guidance on how to try a new practice is given later in this chapter.

Sexual Problems

Not infrequently in married couples' lives, sexual challenges present themselves. This chapter will spend very little time dealing with them because sexual problems are best addressed by a doctor. With advances in medicine, sexual problems can often be fixed or managed—if given the proper attention and care by a qualified professional.

If sexual problems present themselves in your relationship, there could be many causes. Chief among them are emotional and biological problems. Emotional problems, such as a lack of trust in your relationship, a poor self-image, or even a recent loss of someone important in your life can impact your sexual relationship. The passage of time will help heal some of these wounds; others are better dealt with using the assistance of a professional. Other problems are biological. Some men have difficulty achieving and maintaining an erection, some contend with premature ejaculation, and some women have serious difficulty in achieving orgasm. If you are concerned about your sexual functioning, you should first contact your physician. He or she may treat you directly or may refer you to a sex specialist who can help you achieve a more satisfying sexual relationship by giving you tools to help mitigate your biological challenges. Don't be ashamed or afraid to avail yourself of the services of a professional. Any embarrassment that it causes for you will be outweighed by the reward of a better and stronger sex life!

Infidelity

Unfortunately, as we see all too often in today's society, the imperative of faithfulness given in the Seventh Commandment ("You shall not commit adultery") and the love and passion of one's wedding day sometimes fail to last throughout one's life. Why are people unfaithful to one another? How can you try to prevent infidelity from encroaching on your relationship? Nothing is foolproof of course, but this section will seek to explain why people sometimes cheat on their partners and how you, as a couple, can try to protect yourselves from infidelity.

There are many kinds of unfaithfulness, but two will be dealt with in detail here—sexual and emotional unfaithfulness—with the greatest emphasis on sexual infidelity. In heterosexual relationships, research shows that men and women have different fears that are believed to be biologically based. Men's fears about infidelity are most pronounced in the area of sexual infidelity. This is because men psychologically deal with an issue called paternity uncertainty:

> [A] reproductive difference between the sexes is that a woman always knows for sure whether or not a particular child is hers. By comparison, a man suffers paternity uncertainty; unless he is completely confident that his mate has been faithful to him, he cannot be absolutely certain that her child is his. Perhaps for that reason, the same men who consider promiscuous women to be desirable partners in casual relationships often prefer chaste women as partners when they wed.[114]

In the ancient world, no man wanted to support another man's child and the only way to guarantee that his child was his own was if his wife was sexually faithful to him. Women, on the other hand, are most threatened by emotional infidelity. In the not-too-distant past, a woman would be dependent on her husband for her survival. If her husband were to fall for another woman and shift his emotional allegiance to this new woman, his wife would be left without support. "[M]en may experience the most jealousy at the thought of *sexual* infidelity in their mates, whereas women react more to the threat of *emotional* infidelity, the possibility that their partners are falling in love with someone else."[115]

Infidelity often arises because of some large unfulfilled need in the marriage:

> Infidelity is usually a symptom of a troubled marriage. It's easy to point to the infidelity and say, "That's the problem." But most of the time, there is an underlying problem in the relationship. If you or your spouse has turned to someone else, it means that something big is missing from your marriage. And it was probably missing *before* the affair started.[116]

Perhaps it is a lack of sexual fulfillment that drives a person to an affair, but it need not be a sexual problem in a marriage. It can be an emotional problem as well—particularly for women:

> When … it is the wife who is extramaritally involved, it is usually—though certainly not always—due to a *hunger* for emotional intimacy rather than a wish to avoid it. The wife is someone who, hopelessly outdistanced in her emotional pursuit, has given up the chase and gone outside the marriage to find what the husband will not give her—acceptance, validation of her worth, the willingness to listen to her talk about *who she is, as a person,* and learn about *what she needs and wants.*[117]

The best defense against infidelity, therefore, is to work on creating a strong and healthy relationship in and out of the bedroom. A strong relationship provides couples with more than they could ever find looking outside their relationship.

It is important to distinguish between fantasy and reality in this discussion, however. It is a natural and human response to have fantasies:

> Some people believe that fantasies of infidelity are a symptom of an unhappy marriage … Sexual fantasies are a normal part of adulthood, and the desire to have an affair is part of the human condition, especially in today's sexually exciting milieu. At one time or another, everyone imagines having sex with a stranger, covets the lusty neighbor down the street, or daydreams about going to bed with Sharon Stone or Tom Cruise. The only thing new about sexual fantasies is that now women are more open about discussing them. It's just not true that men want sex and women want love—both sexes want sex .[118]

When one moves out of the realm of fantasy and into the realm of reality, things get more dangerous. When instead of an unattainable figure, your fantasies are about your coworker, your neighbor, or your friend, it is a time for caution. By being careful and conscious of the relationships with people outside your marriage, you best protect yourself from the dangers of infidelity.

Infidelity is a serious matter and a threat to any relationship. Perhaps the most succinct advice to keep in mind to defend your relationship against infidelity is expressed by David Mace:

> Many years ago, I read a book on marriage by the famous French writer Andre Maurois, in which he summed this up rather neatly. He spoke of the years in which people date each other and rate each other, and then, in the fullness of time, they make their choice of the one they want to marry. Now they have reached a turning point in life. If they know what they are doing and are serious about it, they will say, "I have chosen; from now on my aim will be, not to search for someone who will please me, but to please the one I have chosen."[119]

A Closing Exercise

Rather than close this discussion of sex with sexual problems and infidelity, I would like to share with you an exercise to help strengthen your relationship. It is an exercise that allows you to get to know your partner's sexual preferences and allows you to develop a sexual relationship that is fulfilling to you both:

With your partner, set aside an afternoon or an evening to talk about the following issues and concerns:

> **Kissing:** Since the beginning of history, kissing has been regarded as an art. But what do we really know about our partner's desires? Ask your partner about how he or she would like to be kissed. What forms of kissing turn her off? Does he like to be kissed firmly or gently? How long do you like to kiss? Where do you like—and dislike—to be kissed? Talk about your first kiss, your most erotic kiss, and the worst and funniest experience you've had when kissing someone else. Then kiss your partner and reappraise your skill.

> **Holding and Hugging:** Have a conversation with your partner about being hugged and held. How much do you like to be held, in what ways, and for how long? What are the best and worst times of the day or night to be held? If holding or hugging feels uncomfortable, talk about your

89

feelings and concerns. At the conclusion of your dialogue, ask your partner how he or she would like to be held tonight.

Touching: There are many ways to touch. Find out what your partner's likes and dislikes are. Does she like to be lightly tickled and stroked? Does he like to be massaged? What parts of your body do you enjoy—and not enjoy—having touched? What are the best times to be touched, and when does touch feel like an intrusion? When you have finished this conversation, make an appointment with your partner to spend an hour exploring each other's body with touch.

Sex: Ask your partner what you can do to make sex more enjoyable and meaningful. Talk about your sexual histories: how you felt about sex when you were young, the negative experiences you may have had, and how you felt about sex when you and your partner first met. What were your childhood fantasies and fears? Share with your partner your best sexual experience together and talk about what made it so special for you. Finally, ask your partner what he or she would like to explore the next time you sexually embrace.[120]

This is not always an easy discussion to begin. We are not used to discussing our sexual likes and dislikes in this way. I encourage you to give it a try, however, since letting your partner know your likes and dislikes and learning about his or hers can only strengthen the physical bond you already share!

Children

As we learned in the section above, procreation is an important commandment in Jewish tradition, as is *sh'lom bayit*, peace in the home. In liberal Jewish tradition, informed choice is also a value—learning about particular rituals and deciding whether and how to integrate these rituals into your life. With these three values in mind, we introduce the discussion of whether or not to have children.

The function of procreation is beautifully stated by the midrash. "According to the Sages, God intentionally left Creation incomplete; in so doing He bestowed upon His creatures the ability to continue the divine process of Creation through procreation."[121] The idea of procreation is even older than the midrash, however. It is the first commandment given to humankind; in Genesis 1:28, we are told that we should "be fruitful and multiply." Based on this verse, it is viewed as a *mitzvah* (religious obligation) for a couple to have children:

> "Be fruitful and multiply," the biblical injunction, is God's most fundamental command to human beings. It is a basic Jewish idea that children created in fulfillment of that command constitute the most significant legacy a person can leave after his sojourn on earth.

> To fulfill the command of procreation, a Jew must bring at least one male and one female child into the world. This *mitzvah* is usually listed as the very first biblical precept binding upon the Jews. *Sefer HaHinuch,* the thirteenth-century compendium of precepts and their rational basis (usually attributed to R. Aaron HaLevi of Barcelona) teaches:

> The purpose of the *mitzvah* is that the world that God wants to be inhabited will indeed be populated. As it is written: "He did not create the world to be a waste; He fashioned it to be a habitation." And this is a most important *mitzvah,* for through it all the other commandments may be fulfilled. For indeed, the *mitzvot* were given to humans to fulfill and not to the angels.[122]

According to this understanding of procreation, having children is the ultimate *mitzvah*, for it allows you to fulfill the command of the *V'ahavta* and teach God's laws to your children and to fulfill the command to tell of the Jewish people's Exodus from Egypt at the Passover Seder.[123]

This command to procreate is not the only thing that should be taken into consideration when deciding whether to have children, however. A secure and stable *bayit* in which both partners are aware of the impact of a child on their relationship is an essential foundation for people deciding to become parents:

> We can safely say that parenthood is an extraordinary and often marvelous adventure, but it is unquestionably

> hard on the relationship between the parents; children
> are endless work, and most parents experience a steep
> and unexpected decline in the time they spend having
> fun together (Kurdek, 1993). When babies arrive,
> conflict increases and satisfaction with the marriage ...
> decrease[s], especially among women (Belsky, 1990). If
> the parents don't expect such difficulties, they're going to
> be surprised.[124]

It is important to realize—before deciding to become parents—that parenting is hard work and the decision to become parents should not be taken lightly. Be careful however not to put the decision off for too long. It is easy to get wrapped up in one's career and not make time to have children. By the time some decide that they want to have children, it may have become more difficult to conceive. That's why it is important to have this discussion now—early in your relationship—so you can plan ahead to maximize your chances for having the number of children you want.

Some people view a child as a way to fix a troubled relationship. *This is a big mistake!* It is taxing on a couple's relationship to have a child—even when the relationship is stable. It is wise to have good communication patterns in place *before* having children since there will be so much more to do after a child arrives that it will be even harder to establish a strong relationship after a child arrives.

The final piece to consider is your own opinion. Do you want to have children? While Jewish tradition ascribes great significance to procreation, it recognizes that procreation is not the only purpose of marriage:

> The procreation of children is a basic goal in marriage, but
> it is not the only one. It is noteworthy that, in the Bible, Eve
> is created for Adam before procreation is contemplated,
> while they are still in the Garden of Eden. The second
> function of marriage is that of companionship. Actually,
> it is the only motive assigned in the creation of a helpmate
> for Adam: "It is not good for man to dwell alone; I will
> make a helper fit for him." (Gen. 2:18)[125]

Having children is something that the two of you should agree to before getting pregnant. This can be an area of considerable tension in a relationship if one person (usually the female) wants children sooner and wants more children than does the other partner. Use your best communication skills with your partner and if you still find yourselves at an impasse, seek professional help to guide you to a fair and comfortable compromise.

Jewish Genetic Testing

Before you have children, it is important to be tested to see whether one or both of you are carriers of the most common genetic diseases in the Jewish community. You should look back in your family history for signs of genetic disease and get tested for those diseases. At the least, you should be tested for Tay-Sachs disease. Only one of you needs to be tested unless that person is found to be a carrier, since both partners need to be carriers in order for the disease to be transmitted. A Web site that was operational at the time of this writing gives information on the types of Jewish genetic diseases and other information about them: http://www.mazornet.com/genetics/index.asp. Use this or another source of information to learn more about these diseases and take the necessary precautions to know as much about them as possible. Knowing in advance whether or not you or your partner is a carrier of any of these diseases may help you make an informed choice about whether or not to have children, and to be prepared for challenges you might face.

Infertility

Despite all the planning about when to have children, it is possible that there will be unforeseen difficulties. It is, unfortunately, not a given that once you decide to have a child that you will be able to do so. Sometimes it takes several months of trying before all the tiny miracles that need to happen in order for a pregnancy to begin occur. Other times, however, there is a more serious problem. Usually after a year of unsuccessfully trying to get pregnant, it is time to consult an infertility specialist. The specialist will test both partners to see what might be causing the difficulty in conception and help you to achieve your dream. Infertility testing is quite expensive, but it is allowing couples who a generation ago could not have gotten pregnant to conceive and give birth to healthy children and part or all of it may be covered by your insurance. In some cases, it is impossible for a couple to conceive, in which case, other alternatives are available should you still want children. Talk with your doctor about adoption and other alternatives that might be available to you.

There are many other issues that come into play when there is difficulty conceiving or carrying a baby. Individuals or couples often battle with issues of self-esteem, a general doubt as to one's self worth. Some become depressed as something that was supposed to be so natural is proving to be so hard. Many people will also begin to doubt their sexual ability. These emotions are powerful, painful, and *normal* in these difficult situations. It is a very vulnerable time. It is vitally important to stay close to your partner—and to talk out your feelings with him or her and/or with a professional. It is also important to be aware that these feelings of shame and inadequacy that accompany this challenging period are major risk factors for an affair to develop. It is important to be vigilant to ensure that you remain faithful to your spouse! Whatever insecurities difficulty getting pregnant may cause, it is important to remember the words of Exodus Rabbah 46:5: "One who raises a child is called 'Parent,' not one just the ones who gave birth to it."

Religious Observance

In a marriage guide such as this, one might expect to see an entire chapter devoted to interfaith marriages. However, since so many of the issues that are important for interfaith couples to address are important for all couples to discuss, the issues for interfaith couples are included in this section and addressed to all couples. There are, of course, some unique issues for interfaith couples to discuss regarding religious observance, but most often, same-faith couples need to have these discussions too. The difference lies in the *degree* to which those issues are present for interfaith couples. Interfaith couples will have to deal with the issues raised in this section in a deeper way. As a result, several comments specifically directed to interfaith couples are included here.

My belief in the need for Jewish couples to discuss religious observance in the same way that interfaith couples do is encapsulated in the title of a book consulted for this work: *Two Jews Can Still Be a Mixed Marriage*.

> When a Jew marries a Christian, everyone expects numerous emotionally charged conflicts and negotiations related to religious observance. No one is surprised if the couple gets into heated debate about how to observe the holidays or if they have trouble creating a wedding ceremony that satisfies both sides of the family. I read in a book on intermarriage the following misleading statement about a Jew who married a Christian: "Had they fallen in love with another Jew, they might never have had to reexamine their feelings about Judaism. Those emotions heat up in the crucible of an intermarriage, where they

feel their identities are threatened." The author of that piece clearly hadn't spoken to enough Jewish couples or he would have realized that religious conflict is not a stranger to Jewish marriages.

> Every marriage, even between two Jews, is an intermarriage between two individuals with different souls and backgrounds.[126]

Any marriage, this quote makes clear, is a merging of two different experiences and therefore two different desires and expectations as to what kinds and what level of observance a couple will have in their home.

You should not be surprised that this book advocates Jewish ritual and Jewish rhythms in your life as a couple, but you may be surprised to read the following:

> It's one of those statistics that catches your eye and makes you say "No, that can't be!" But according to a groundbreaking Gallup survey, happiness in a marriage is better predicted by how often a couple prays together than by how often they make love.[127]

Your ability to develop a ritual observance that is comfortable to you both will help strengthen your relationship! One example of a ritual that Judaism provides that allows for this strengthening is Shabbat. "Nothing is potentially more enriching for marriage and the family than a modern observance of Shabbat in the spirit of the Jewish tradition."[128] The Jewish ritual of Shabbat long preceded Masters and Johnson's famous twentieth century work on the sexual function and dysfunction of the human male and female, so we see the wisdom of Judaism's ancient tradition when we read:

> The Sabbath provides a clear corrective to a problem that William Masters and Virginia Johnson cite in *The Pleasure Bond:*
>
> There is a danger of letting everyday chores and responsibilities come between you as husband and wife, so that you are always postponing the pleasure of having each other's company because there is work to be done.

> It would probably amaze you to know how many husbands and wives become sexually dysfunctional as a result of the so-called work ethic.[129]

Of course there are many different things you can choose to do—or not do—in your observance of any particular ritual. Taking Shabbat as our example, you can choose to do however many of the items on the following the list of Shabbat observances that you see fit—or you can choose to add some of your own:

- Light Shabbat candles
- Say the blessings over *challah* and wine
- Bless each other
- Bless the children
- Attend Friday night services
- Attend Saturday morning services
- Refrain from doing chores
- Take a walk
- Welcome in the new week with *Havdalah*

There are many other rituals around which you as a couple will need to figure out your desired level of observance. One example is *nidda*, but there are many other rituals of Jewish life that you could incorporate into your lives. You could make a practice of regularly attending synagogue together. Or, perhaps you would like to read a Jewish book or study a Jewish text together. Maybe you would like to explore *kashrut*, keeping kosher, and see if and how you would like to involve that practice in your lives. You could also adopt traditional customs or create your own to help you observe Jewish holidays.

In order to determine what kind of religious life you want to lead, it helps to reflect on a few questions with your partner. Use the following questions as a guide for beginning a conversation about the kind of religious life that you would like to have in your home.

Heavenly Thoughts

Spiritual beliefs hold the key to many relational values, but couples often take such values for granted and thus do not talk in depth to each other about what they mean. By exploring your partner's spiritual beliefs, you can help each other to live more closely to the values you honor and respect. This sentence-completion game will help you to initiate a heavenly conversation or two. Take turns responding to the following sentence stems—and then talk about the feelings they bring up:

- As a child, what I loved most about religion was …
- As a child, what I disliked most about religion was …
- My parents dealt with religion and spirituality by …
- When growing up, my favorite religious stories were …
- When growing up, my least favorite biblical stories were …
- If I could change one thing about the religion I was raised in, I would …
- My current spiritual beliefs are …
- My beliefs about God are …
- The most difficult issue for me concerning spirituality and religion is …
- The spiritual values I want to develop more fully are …
- The religious values I find most restrictive are …
- If I were God, I would …
- If I could add three new Commandments, they would be …
- My favorite rituals we observed when growing up were …
- My favorite rituals that I currently practice are …[130]

Interfaith couples need to have further discussion about the place of the two religions in the home. This series of questions can provide a jumping-off point for your conversation about what this marriage means for your religious life as a couple.

- The most important part of my religion to me is …
- The thing I like least about my own religion is …
- The thing I like least about my partner's religion is …
- If it were up to me, our involvement with my religion …
- The thing that makes me most uncomfortable about my partner's religion is …
- As a child, religion to me was …
- My favorite holiday is …
- My favorite religious experience was …
- When I don't celebrate a holiday, I feel …
- If my children weren't raised in my religion, I would feel …[131]

Additionally, should you decide—and be blessed with the ability—to have children, you will need to determine what kind of religious upbringing they should receive. If you have a boy, would he have a *b'rit milah*—a ritual circumcision—or if you have a girl, would she have a naming ceremony? Do you want your child(ren) to go to religious school? Do you want your child to have a bar/bat mitzvah? Do you want them to go to Jewish summer camp? All of these issues—and many more—will be present in your life whether you are a couple made up of two Jews or whether you are in a mixed marriage.

Interfaith couples face additional challenges, however. Interfaith couples must decide which religion to follow, or to attempt to raise their children in both faiths or with none at all. They also must deal with issues of the Jewish status of their children. As regards the issue whether to raise a child in one faith or in both, interview research with children of interfaith marriages suggests that children prefer their parents to raise them in one faith or another:

> They valued clarity and a sense of security. They felt parents should choose a religious identity for the children and not leave it up to them to choose. Furthermore, they thought parents should furnish an environment in which the children would feel comfortable living with that identity.

> They wanted roots in one of their parents' religions and cultures, but branches extended to the other's. Indeed, many of the children we talked with were troubled that one parent had suppressed all traces of his or her own religious heritage and culture. In many cases, the children had felt compelled to follow the few clues they had found about this past and sought to re-create that hidden identity for themselves.[132]

However, children do not only want a decision about which faith they will be raised in. Children ask more from interfaith parents: "Those children who seem to feel best about growing up in interfaith families have almost inevitably been raised by parents who are themselves comfortable with their own religious identities, whatever they may be."[133]

The other question that interfaith couples must discuss and come to some understanding about is the Jewish status of their child. According to *halacha*, Jewish law, a child is Jewish if he or she is born to a Jewish *mother*. This is the definition used by the Orthodox and Conservative movements of Judaism. If the father of the child is Jewish and the mother is not, even if they are raising the child as a Jew, according to Jewish law, the child is not a Jew unless he has converted. It is easiest to convert an infant at birth and allow her to be recognized as a Jew by the entire Jewish world because it is harder to convert once one becomes an adult. In Reform Judaism, a child is considered Jewish if one of his parents is Jewish and the child is being raised and educated exclusively as a Jew. This means that in the case given above, according to the Reform movement, the child is a Jew, but that child's religious status is not recognized by the other two major movements. This may turn out to be a non-issue for the child, but should he or she fall in love with a Conservative or Orthodox Jew, there would be problems since the child would not be considered a Jew within those movements without conversion.

Of course, the views that you hold in anticipation of marriage might not be the views that you hold when you decide to have children. People change. The best that we can do is to be honest with our partners and try to deal with the difficult issues in marriage and childrearing in a way that strengthens our relationships and leads to a deeper love between partners.

Trying New Rituals

How do you know if a ritual will be meaningful for you? Trying new rituals is the same as trying anything new. Sometimes you try something and it feels right the first time you do it. You wonder why you never tried doing this before! Other times, it takes longer. Sometimes the first several times you do something it seems a bit strange—after all, it is something you haven't done before. After a while, it may begin to feel more comfortable—and more meaningful—to you. Try to think of something that you've tried that fits into each of these categories.

Just as new things sometimes take some getting used to, so too do rituals. Sometimes we try rituals and immediately know that the ritual is something that we want to include in our practice. Other times, we may try a ritual and it might not feel comfortable the first time we do it. But just as we aren't always comfortable with the new things we try, we may not be immediately comfortable with new rituals, and need time to grow into them. In time, these rituals may well become important parts of our ritual practice. It is, therefore, important not to dismiss rituals as meaningless after trying them once. It is better to try new rituals several times before evaluating whether you would like to include them in your regular practice. For example, the first time you go to services, it might not seem to be something you'd want to include in your regular practice, but as you get to know people, learn the melodies, and grow to appreciate the way that it makes Shabbat different from the rest of the week, you may come to appreciate going to services and make it a regular part of your life. It is, of course, possible that you may try a ritual and find that it has no meaning for you, but you should not dismiss rituals before giving them a chance!

Conclusion

We have seen throughout this chapter that building a *bayit* is hard work. There are many things that go into the construction and maintenance of a house. Yet it is worth it, for the home that you build is the place you come to be with the one with whom you have chosen to share your life. May it be a place that reflects your values and your passions.

Chapter 6:
Tying it All Together

In Chapter 1, we learned that the Jewish wedding ceremony was once two separate ceremonies—the first being the ceremony of engagement or betrothal, in Hebrew called *eirusin*. It was at this time that the couple declared their intention to marry. Plans would then begin for the second ceremony, which was held several months to a year later. In this second ceremony, the couple was formally married; in Hebrew this ceremony is called *nisuin*.

In some respects, it seems quite strange—in the Jewish wedding ceremony, engagement and marriage now happen on the same day. Why, one might well ask, do we need *eirusin* at all? A Biblical text that is often used in wedding ceremonies helps us answer this question. Hosea 2:21 describes God's promise to Israel:

> And I shall betroth you to Me forever;
> And I shall betroth you to Me with righteousness and
> justice, with kindness and mercy;
> And I shall betroth you to Me in faithfulness.

The relationship between partners is often seen as a parallel to the relationship between God and Israel.

> "Human marriage should, at least to some extent, mirror
> the ideal of the relationship between God and Israel. A
> husband should be to God as his wife is to Israel. As
> the relationship between God and Israel is covenantal,

specifying mutual obligations, so too should human marriage be reciprocal."[134]

So, then, if we understand these words from the *eirusin* service as inspiring us to specify those obligations that we take on by committing ourselves to another, how are we to understand the quotation from Hosea? What are we promising to do for one another when we use this verse in our wedding ceremonies? One source understands it this way:

1. "And I shall betroth you to Me forever." This refers to an eternal, unconditional bond. It is "love which is independent of any external factor," free of any physical influence and elevated above all fluctuations in life. It is not an aesthetic experience of a transient nature, but an eternal bond.

2. As a result, "And I shall betroth you to Me with righteousness and justice, with kindness and mercy." This strong union expresses itself through virtuous behavior. The four qualities quoted above are some of the basic attributes by which divine goodness is revealed in this world: "There are seven attributes which serve to establish the throne of God [in this world]: Faith, righteousness, justice, kindness, mercy, truth, and peace." On the one hand, "righteousness and justice"—complete integrity with the full force of law and truth—are essential, but on the other hand, "kindness and mercy"—love, affection, peace, and friendship—are also necessary.

3. Above all, "And I shall betroth you to Me in faithfulness." This verse implies the devotion, the belonging to each other, the inner unity, and the love of one soul for the other. [135]

The first half of the wedding service is all about the promises we make to our partners. It would be easy to see this as entering into a contract with our beloved. After all, couples sign a *ketubah* at the wedding, which has its roots as a financial protection for the woman in the event of the dissolution of the relationship. Yet to view marriage as merely a contractual relationship is to shortchange it. Maurice Lamm helps take us beyond the idea of a strictly contractual relationship to something deeper and far more significant. "The Jewish concept of marriage can be summarized as follows: The form, the contract, and the process are contractual. The content, the bond, and the resulting relationship are covenantal."[136] Soon after, he clarifies the difference between a contractual and a covenantal relationship. "By contract, we share duties; by covenant, we share destinies."[137]

Over the last several chapters, you have begun to consider what is important to you as a couple. Around what values and commitments do you want to build your relationship? What do you want the world to know about you? Even though we use traditional prayers that have been used for generations, your wedding can—and should—be a time when your family and friends learn about what is important to the two of you. There are many places in the wedding ceremony and in your life as a married couple where your priorities can shine through. They become evident in the choices that you make with regards to the rituals brought up in Chapter 1. They come through in the people you choose to honor by asking them to participate in your marriage. They come through in the additional words you might write for or read at your wedding—reflecting ideas and values that are particular to you as a couple and to your relationship.

Just as importantly, they come through in how you choose to include the values that have been presented in the previous chapters in your wedding ceremony. These values are important stepping-stones to a deep and meaningful relationship. It is worth taking time to remind yourselves of the values that this book has presented and to begin to think about how these values will be reflected in your wedding ceremony and in your life together.

Chapter 2 focused on *dorot*. We talked about how your family of origin influences you. Your family of origin was where you first learned about marriage and what it meant to be in relationship with another person. In some cases, this example was positive, leading you to want to replicate those warm feelings in your own relationship. In other cases, the example was negative, giving you ideas of what you would want to do differently in your relationship with your partner. We talked about the changes in your relationship with family and friends that marriage causes as you make your spouse your number one priority; we talked about how to prepare yourself and those you love for those changes. We talked about your relationship with your partner's parents and a few tips to keep that relationship positive and constructive. Finally, we spent some time beginning to dream about the future of your relationship. Now, is a good time to revisit your goals and dreams and see if there are any changes you would like to make.

Putting the Value of *Dorot* into Your Ceremony

1. Offer a blessing of thanks to your parents for what they have given to you. (Even if you have a troubled relationship with

one or both of them, there are still things for which you can thank them!)
2. Honor your parents and friends by offering ways for them to participate in your marriage ceremony.
3. Talk with your rabbi about one thing that he or she could share about what each of you is bringing from your family of origin into your marriage.

Including the Value of *Dorot* in Your New Marriage

1. Set up a way to keep in touch with family and friends on a regular basis.
2. Devise ways to include your family in your new life together.
3. Plant a tree in Israel in honor of your families and all they have done to nourish you.

In Chapter 3, we were introduced to the who, what, where, when, why, and how of communication and conflict. We learned how important good patterns of communication are to creating a strong and healthy relationship, and we discussed some techniques to make sure that you are able to create these good patterns in your relationship. The values that shaped that chapter were *emet* and *emunah*—truth and faithfulness. We saw how important it is to share our feelings with our partner without having to say everything that comes to our minds. We saw how important it is to be sensitive to our partners—even in the midst of disagreements—by trying to express displeasure and criticism with as much compassion, care, and love as we can muster. We also saw how important it is to listen to our partners and to try to understand what they are trying to say to us so that we can adequately respond to their needs.

Putting the Values of *Emet* and *Emunah* into Your Ceremony

1. Have the vows you write to each other reflect the importance of both sharing your feelings with your partner and maintaining your individuality.
2. Articulate to each other a commitment to your marriage and a willingness to work hard (for it is hard work!) to deal with differences and disagreements.

3. Begin your marriage on the right foot by sharing the excitement and the anxiety that you are feeling as your wedding day approaches—and on the wedding day—by listening openly and intently as your partner shares with you his or her thoughts.

Including the Values of *Emet* and *Emunah* in Your New Marriage

1. Set aside time to discuss your feelings. Don't let them bottle up inside you for very long because unacknowledged annoyances and hurts can quickly turn into resentment!
2. Periodically (once every six months or so) do a communication checkup. Talk with each other about the ways in which you communicate with each other. When your ability to communicate well with each other decreases, it is time to pay serious attention to rebuilding effective communication.
3. Revise your love statement to reflect your changing hopes and dreams.

In Chapter 4, we discussed the two kinds of bank accounts—emotional and financial—using the value of responsibility, *acharayut*. We looked at how to make sure that there was a positive balance in each account on a daily basis by making sure the deposits we make outweigh the withdrawals. We discussed how to keep a positive balance over the short-term by building up a credit of goodwill and some saved money to help weather a rough time. Finally, we discussed how to plan for the long-term by investing money to plan for retirement and by investing in your friendship with your partner.

Putting the Value of *Acharayut* into Your Ceremony

1. Donate some money to *tzedakah* in honor of your wedding as a way to let this moment of great happiness for you bring happiness to people in need.
2. Write a paragraph or two to read to your partner during the ceremony about why you love him or her.
3. Try to forgive each other for the hurts that you carry around from earlier in your relationship and start your marriage with an even greater positive balance in your emotional bank account!

Including the Value of *Acharayut* in Your New Marriage

1. Establish a practice of giving *tzedakah* on a regular basis to causes about which you are passionate.
2. Challenge yourself to do one nice thing (that you might not ordinarily do) for your spouse each and every day.
3. Invest time in finding out what is meaningful for your partner as a show of affection and do whatever that may be.
4. Work on crafting a reasonable budget for the two of you that balances the needs of spenders and savers.

In the previous chapter, we discussed certain aspects of your home life—the things that make up your *bayit*. We talked about the importance of an equitable division of chores so that both of you are contributing to the building and maintenance of your home. We talked about the importance of developing a healthy sexual relationship, not measured by what statistics or television tells you that you should be doing, but rather by doing what leaves the two of you feeling fulfilled, satisfied, and connected to each other. We began the discussion of whether or not you want to have children, one that ideally you will continue to have in the months and years to come. Finally, we discussed religious observance and the importance of coming up with a religious practice that is meaningful to you.

Putting the Value of *Bayit* into Your Ceremony

1. Make explicit to the friends and family that have gathered to celebrate with you that just as they were invited to your wedding to see you underneath the *chupah*, so too are they invited to your home after you get married.
2. Think about the message of the *chupah*, open on the sides, but providing shelter and privacy above. Think about how this "home" symbolizes the home you will make with your partner.
3. See how the rituals of the wedding ceremony provide a structure to your wedding. Think about how to incorporate rituals into your lives after the wedding, perhaps even incorporating these values into your *ketubah*.

Including the Value of *Bayit* in Your New Marriage

1. Work on creating a sexual relationship that satisfies both of your needs. This means that you need to be open and honest with your partner and yourself about what you want.
2. Begin creating a home that, like the ancient Temple in Jerusalem, can be a place of sacred encounter with God. Let it be a place, through discussion and ritual, where the presence of the Divine is welcome.
3. Strive to make your home a *beit k'nesset* (house of assembly or synagogue), *beit sefer* (house of the book or school), and a *beit t'filah* (house of prayer or sanctuary). Let your home be a place where Judaism is explored through community, study, and a relationship with God.

Your wedding is a very important day in your lives. It is a day that you may have been dreaming about for many years—one that you certainly have been planning for a long time. It is a time of great transition. Your relationship is about to attain new permanence, to be elevated to that of a covenantal bond. It is only natural that the wedding day be viewed as such an important day! It is not, however, the most important day that you will share as a married couple. The most important day that you share as a couple is every day you two are together. It is every day that you participate in that covenantal relationship with your partner. Your wedding is a kickoff to every other day in your married life.

Our time together has nearly come to an end. I hope you have achieved a greater insight into yourself and your partner. I hope you have learned some skills that will help you continue to grow as a couple and allow you to develop a strong and healthy relationship. I hope you have learned that a good marriage is not easy; it requires constant care and attention in order to flourish to its full potential. I hope that you have learned that the rituals you incorporate into your home are important. I hope you will remember that every relationship has its rough spots—its times of tension and quarrel— that are only natural with the merging of two distinct individuals into this precious and tight bond, and that patience and care is necessary to weather these tough times. I hope you will remember that you are not alone. If you are having trouble making your marriage all that you want it to be, there are people who can help you get your marriage back on track and you should not be embarrassed or reluctant to turn to them to help you. Your partner and your marriage are truly special things in your life and you should fight hard to make the most of your marriage!

If you remember these lessons, this venture has been a success. If these lessons become part of who you are—as an individual *and* as a couple—then your relationship will stand a good chance of growing healthy and strong over the years. As Pirke Avot teaches us, *"V'lo hamidrash ha'ikar ela hama'aseh*—Not the teaching is paramount, but rather the action thereon."[138]

I would like to offer you two Jewish phrases used at times of conclusion as wishes for your marriage. The first is the one that you will hear a lot on your wedding day, *mazal tov,* which loosely translated means "good luck." I wish you the best of luck as you embark on a life-long journey of learning about—and from—each other. I pray that it is a rewarding one. The other phrase of conclusion is offered to someone who has completed a difficult task. We wish them *yashar koakh,* which we can translate as "good strength." You are now about to complete the difficult task of preparing logistically, emotionally, and intellectually for marriage. You have also completed this book. For your efforts, we wish you *yashar koakh* as you embark on the wonderful and challenging adventure of marriage!

Bibliography

The Aleph-Bet of Marriage. A curriculum produced by the Union for Reform Judaism (URJ) to be implemented in small groups of couples preparing for marriage, facilitated by a social worker (and a rabbi at some sessions).

Arond, Miriam and Pauker, M.D., Samuel L.. *The First Year of Marriage* New York: Warner Books, 1987. A good, if slightly dated, discussion. However, the book is not well written so some ideas get lost. Contains lots of case examples and diagnostic tests. The tests are better than most since they don't score you, but rather suggest that you discuss any issues that come up.

Aviner, Rabbi Shlomo. *Dimensions of Love*. Jerusalem: Urim Publications, 2000. A relatively traditional account that is brief and accessible (i.e. Hebrew terms are often defined, etc.). The book has several good passages.

Bass, Daniel H. "Premarital Counseling." Diss. Jewish Communal Service, Hebrew Union College, 1982. Written from the perspective of a Jewish Communal Service student, this thesis outlined the state of Jewish premarital counseling in 1980s Los Angeles. It was valuable to read from a social work perspective on this topic.

Benjamin, Robert M. "The Role of the Reform Rabbi in Premarital Counseling." Diss. Rabbinical School, Hebrew Union College, 1966. This thesis represents a survey of rabbis as to what was being done regarding premarital counseling in the 1960s.

Betcher, M.D., William and Macauley, Robbie. *The Seven Basic Quarrels of Marriage*. Toronto: Random House, Inc., 1990. Suggests that most marital strife can be traced back to a basic quarrel among the following issues: gender, loyalties, money, power, sex, privacy, and children. The book is not that well written, but did provide an interesting perspective to consider.

Birner, Dr. Louis. "Unconscious Resistance to Pre-Marital Counseling." *Pre-Marital Counseling*. Ed. Rabbi David M. Feldman. New York: Commission on Synagogue Relations: Federation of Jewish Philanthropies of New York, 1974. 19–26. A pamphlet with brief chapters by various rabbis on the state of premarital counseling in the mid 1970s.

The Book of Legends—Sefer Ha-Aggadah. 1908–1911. Trans. William G. Braude. Ed. Hayim Nahman and Ravnitzky Bialik, Yehoshua Hana. New York: Schocken Books, 1992. A collection of the sages' writings on various topics, including Biblical characters, and rabbinic sages. Also addresses particular topics, some of which were relevant to this research.

Boteach, Shmuley. *Kosher Sex*. New York: Doubleday, 1999. Explores issues of sex and sexuality from a Jewish perspective, although designed to appeal to a broader audience.

Brehm, Sharon S., et al. *Intimate Relationships*. 1985. 3rd ed. New York, NY: McGraw-Hill Higher Education, 2002. A college textbook that summarizes the psychological literature on what makes relationships work or fail. There is a wealth of good information related to marriage. It was a foundational text for this book.

Brothers, Dr. Joyce. *What Every Woman Ought to Know About Love & Marriage*. New York: Simon & Schuster, 1984. Although renowned, the book did not have much to contribute to this research. The age of the book showed as Brothers had an antiquated view of the responsibilities/roles of a woman in marriage.

Buxbaum, Yitzhak. *Jewish Spiritual Practices*. Northvale, New Jersey: Jason Aronson Inc., 1990. A large book that gives the mystical perspective on various topics. For this project, the chapter on sex was consulted. Its perspective of sex as a unification of aspects of the Divine and a drawing close of human and Divine were unique among the works consulted.

Carter, M.S.W., Betty and Peters, Joan. *Love, Honor and Negotiate*. New York: Pocket Books, 1996. Similar in many ways to other books written from a like perspective. Only a few citations used in this research.

Charny, Dr. Israel. *Marital Love & Hate.* New York: The Macmillan Company, 1972. Contains two books, one geared toward psychologists, and the other as a manual for the layperson. Neither was written particularly well, but it provided an interesting idea— that hate is something to be celebrated, not feared, in a marriage.

Coleman, Dr. Paul. *The 30 Secrets of Happily Married Couples*. Holbrook, MA: Bob Adams, Inc., 1992. One among a multitude of books suggesting a key to marital happiness. A few creative suggestions, but most of the ideas are stated better elsewhere.

Covey, Stephen R. *The Seven Habits of Highly Effective People*. New York: Simon & Schuster, 1989. A great book for those seeking to develop their characters as internally motivated, responsible team players. Covey is a strong advocate of principle-based vision statements as the guide for behavior. Covey also writes about the emotional bank account, a principle covered in this book.

Cowan, Paul with Cowan, Rachel. *Mixed Blessings*. New York: Doubleday, 1987. A distillation of what this couple has learned from their own interfaith experience as well as lessons learned from groups that they have facilitated.

Crohn, Joel, Markman, Howard J., Blumberg, Susan L., and Levine, Janice R.. *Fighting for Your Jewish Marriage*. San Francisco: Jossey-Bass, 2000. Tries to address itself to the trend by which Jewish marriages are becoming like all other marriages. It seeks to preserve a Jewish flavor in marriages.

Diamant, Anita. *The New Jewish Wedding*. New York: Fireside, 1985. A standard among Jewish wedding texts. Deals with the traditional ceremony and traditional rituals as well as providing some modern alternatives. Includes some commentary on the reception, although the focus is on the ceremony.

Domestic Abuse Statistics. 24/Feb. 2004 <http://www.chaicolorado.org/statistics.htm>. A resource about domestic abuse for the Jewish community of Colorado that also has some general statistics.

Elster, Rabbi Sheldon. "Values Suggested by the Jewish Wedding Ceremony." *Pre-Marital Counseling.* Ed. Rabbi David M. Feldman. New York: Commission on Synagogue Relations: Federation of Jewish Philanthropies of New York, 1974. 27–30. A pamphlet with brief chapters by various rabbis on the state of premarital counseling in the mid 1970s.

Emerson, James. "The End of a Marriage." *Marriage: An Interfaith Guide for All Couples.* Ed. Rev. Raban Hathorn, et al. New York: Association Press, 1970. 239–48. A book designed to give a "religious" view of marriage, but not from one particular religious perspective. An interesting idea, but the age of the book meant that it was of limited use as the understanding of how to build a successful marriage has advanced considerably since then.

Encyclopedia of Jewish Humor. Ed. Henry D. Spaulding. New York: Jonathan David Publishers, 1969. A treasury of Jewish humor.

Feldman, Rabbi David M. "The Spiritual Dimension." *Pre-Marital Counseling.* Ed. Rabbi David M. Feldman. New York: Commission on Synagogue Relations: Federation of Jewish Philanthropies of New York, 1974. 41–45. A pamphlet with brief chapters by various rabbis on the state of premarital counseling in the mid 1970s.

Friedman, Avraham Peretz. *Marital Intimacy.* Northvale, New Jersey: Jason Aronson, 1996. An exploration of sex and sexuality from a traditional perspective.

Gibran, Kahlil. *The Prophet.* New York: Alfred A. Knopf, 1923. A Lebanese poet who wrote a short poem on marriage that is widely read and used today.

Gittelsohn, Roland B. *The Extra Dimension*. New York: Union of American Hebrew Congregations, 1983. A dated, yet still valuable, perspective on Judaism's teachings regarding marriage.

Gold, Rabbi Michael. *Does God Belong in the Bedroom?* Philadelphia: The Jewish Publication Society, 1992. Elaborates on the Jewish view of sex, focusing particularly on the idea that sex is holy. Promotes the idea that there is a ladder of sexual holiness. Also contains a discussion of sexually related issues such as abortion, homosexuality, and raising sexually responsible children.

Goldman, Marcus Jacob and Goldman, Lori J. *What to Do After You Say "I Do."* Rocklin, California: Prima Publishing, 1998. A general marriage handbook with little to distinguish itself.

Gordis, Robert. *Love & Sex*. New York: Farrar Straus Giroux, 1978. Begins with a discussion of love and sex as understood by Christian theology as that provides the basis for American views of the topics. Includes a discussion of how Judaism's view is different. Concludes with discussions of pressing topics of the day.

Gottman, Ph.D., John M. and Silver, Nan. *The Seven Principles for Making Marriage Work*. New York: Crown Publishers, Inc., 1999. Gottman, one of the world's leading relationship experts, challenges some commonly held beliefs about what makes for a successful marriage. The book provides a lot of important information although at times his writing can appear arrogant.

Goulston, M.D., Mark with Goldberg, Philip. *The 6 Secrets of a Lasting Relationship*. New York: G. P. Putnam's Sons, 2001. Uses the acronym CREATE to stand for the six pillars upon which a successful marriage is built (Chemistry, Respect, Enjoyment, Acceptance, Trust, and Empathy). A well constructed book that gives new terminology for the tools of a successful marriage.

Green, Rabbi Alan S. *Sex, God, and the Sabbath*. Cleveland: Temple Emanu El, 1979. An older book that explores the relationship between the three elements addressed in the title.

Guldner, Th.D., Claude A. "Marriage Preparation and Marriage Enrichment." *Pastoral Psychology* 25.4 (Summer 1977): 248–59. Other articles include "Marriage in Transition: Implications for Social Policy" by David R. Mace.

Harley, Jr., Willard F. *Fall in Love Stay in Love*. Grand Rapids, Michigan: Fleming H. Revell, 2001. Uses the idea of a love bank, an appealing way of looking at emotional balance in a relationship. Puts forward a psychologist's plan for premarital counseling. Some of his concepts are useful; others seemed to be too simplistic.

Hathorn, Rev. Raban, Genne, Rev. William, and Brill, Rabbi Mordecai. "A Final Word and a Prayer." *Marriage: An Interfaith Guide for All Couples*. Ed. Rev. Raban Hathorn, et al. New York: Association Press, 1970. 249. A book designed to give a "religious" view of marriage, but not from one particular religious perspective. An interesting idea, but the age of the book made it of limited use as the understanding of how to build a successful marriage has advanced considerably since then.

Horsley, RN, MFCC, Gloria Call. *The In-Law Survival Manual*. New York: John Wiley & Sons, Inc., 1996. A book on a topic of concern to many couples, how to negotiate and strengthen in-law relationships. It addresses different types of in-laws and stages of an in-law relationship. Much of the advice is very general, suggesting that one should apply the same sensitivity and communication skills with one's in-laws as one does with one's spouse.

Jaffe, Azriella. *Two Jews Can Still Be a Mixed Marriage*. Franklin Lakes, New Jersey: Career Press, 2000. Useful more for the title than for the content. Book talks about different spiritual journeys and conflicts over synagogues, adult study, day school, summer camp, holidays, life cycle, and ritual observance.

The Jewish Marriage Anthology. 1965. Ed. Philip and Hanna Goodman. Philadelphia: The Jewish Publication Society of America, 1971. A collection of Jewish sources from the Bible all the way to the time of publication. Many sections of this text had resources that were of use in the preparation of this book.

Judson, Daniel and Wiener, Nancy H. *Meeting at the Well.* New York: UAHC Press, 2002. Deals with many important issues that engaged couples deal with, including intimacy, finances, and religion. A valuable guide for the period leading up to marriage.

Karotkin, Jennifer. *Press Release: JWI Publications Setting the Standard for Discussion of Domestic Abuse in the Jewish Community.* 23/ September 2002 <http://www.jewishwomen.org/press/2002/0923. htm>. An article that summarizes some of the publications of Jewish Women International in the area of domestic violence.

Kaufman, Michael. *Love, Marriage, and Family in Jewish Law and Tradition.* Northvale, New Jersey: Jason Aronson, Inc., 1992. A handbook on marriage from the traditional Jewish world that brings in many sources. While the conclusions and the perspective differ from this book's orientation, the sources were of great value.

Kinder, Dr. Melvyn and Cowan, Dr. Connell. *Husbands and Wives.* New York: Clarkson N. Potter, Inc., 1989. The book's thrust is to support a self-directed marriage in contrast to an other-directed marriage. They believe that by changing one's own behavior, one can change the functioning of the system without actively trying to change one's partner.

Klagsbrun, Francine. *Voices of Wisdom.* Middle Village, New York: Jonathan David Publishers, Inc., 1980. A wonderful collection of Jewish texts on several topics, including "Relating to Others," "Love, Sex, and Marriage," and "Family Relationships."

Kobliner, Beth. *Get A Financial Life.* New York: Simon & Schuster, 1996. An introduction to the world of financial responsibility. It covers such areas as debt, basic banking, investing, planning for retirement, getting a home, insurance, and taxes. A helpful guide for those taking charge of their own finances for the first time.

Lamm, Maurice. *The Jewish Way in Love and Marriage.* San Francisco: Harper & Row, Publishers, 1980. A classic work on the traditional views of love and marriage.

Landes, Rabbi Aaron. "Sample Interview: Jewish Marriage." *Pre-Marital Counseling.* Ed. Rabbi David M. Feldman. New York: Commission on Synagogue Relations: Federation of Jewish Philanthropies of New York, 1974. 31–40. A pamphlet with brief chapters by various rabbis on the state of premarital counseling in the mid 1970s.

Latner, Helen. *The Everything Jewish Wedding Book.* Holbrook, Massachusetts: Adams Media Corporation, 1998. A book that claims to be a guide to both the ceremony and the reception. In reality, its discussion of the reception seems more substantial.

Lewis, Rabbi Ellen Jay. "Preparing for the *Chupah:* Premarital Counseling." *Jewish Pastoral Care.* Ed. Rabbi Dayle A. Friedman. Woodstock, Vermont: Jewish Lights Publishing, 2001. 205–36. A guide which gives the clergy officiating at the wedding a guide for how to approach premarital counseling. A good introduction to the process of counseling for clergy.

Mace, David and Vera. "What You Build Into Your Marriage." *Marriage: An Interfaith Guide for All Couples.* Ed. Rev. Raban Hathorn, et al. New York: Association Press, 1970. 52–94. A book designed to give a "religious" view of marriage, but not from one particular religious perspective. An interesting idea, but the age of the book made it of limited use as the understanding of how to build a successful marriage has advanced considerably since then.

Mace, David R. *Close Companions.* New York: The Continuum Publishing Company, 1982. Builds the case for marriage enrichment. An interesting study on what is being done and what isn't, what works and what doesn't in the field of marriage preparation and defense. The discussion of marriage encounter was interesting, but not directly relevant to this research.

—. *Getting Ready for Marriage.* Nashville: Abingdon Press, 1972. One of the leading marriage counselors of the late twentieth century writes a book for the public about what his premarital conversations look like. The book contains a lot of valuable information.

Marcus, Eric. *Together Forever.* New York: Anchor Books by Doubleday, 1998. This book is mostly interviews. Therefore it only contains a few items that apply to this research.

Neuman, M. Gary. *Emotional Infidelity.* New York: Crown Publishers, 2001. The book's content is far better represented by the tag line: "How to affair-proof your marriage." It has lots of good information although some of the suggestions were not realistic, such as avoiding friendships with people of the opposite sex.

Neurotica. Ed. Melvin Jules Bukiet. New York: W. W. Norton & Company, 1999. A collection of chapters, sections of works, short stories, or plays that in one way or another deal with sex. Although interesting, there were very few selections that fit in with this work.

Olitzky, Rabbi Kerry M. *Making a Successful Jewish Interfaith Marriage.* Woodstock, Vermont: Jewish Lights Publishing, 2003. Addresses many of the issues that any couple needs to face regarding relating to family and religious observance from the perspective of interfaith marriages, where the issues are often more pronounced.

Petsonik, Judy and Remsen, Jim. *The Intermarriage Handbook.* New York: William Morrow and Company, Inc., 1988. A detailed treatment of issues that arise in interfaith couples' lives. In particular, the book focuses on difficulties with parents, the challenge of different ethnic backgrounds, how to negotiate holiday observance, and determining how to raise the children.

Pietropinto, M.D. Anthony and Simenauer, Jacqueline. *Husbands and Wives.* New York: Times Books, 1979. Although a bit older, the book was still useful. There were a lot of quotations from survey participants which are irrelevant to this research, but the patterns that emerged are still of value.

Pre-Marital Counseling. Ed. Rabbi David M. Feldman. New York: Commission on Synagogue Relations: Federation of Jewish Philanthropies of New York, 1974. A pamphlet with brief chapters by various rabbis on the state of premarital counseling in the mid 1970s.

The Pre-Marital Interview. Ed. Barbara Trainin. New York: Federation of Jewish Philanthropies of New York Commission on Synagogue Relations Task Force on Marriage and Divorce, 1983.

The Rabbinical Assembly Rabbi's Manual. New York: The Rabbinical Assembly, 1998. A two-volume work. The first volume deals with, among other topics, the marriage ceremony. It contains the traditional service as well as some modern alternatives.

Reuben, Steven Carr. *But How Will You Raise the Children?* New York: Pocket Books, 1987. Based on the author's counseling experience, the book addresses the major challenges that interfaith couples face as well as some items of generic value in terms of constructing a healthy relationship. A good resource for interfaith couples.

Rich, Hilary, and Kravitz, M.D., Helama Laks. *The Complete Idiot's Guide to the Perfect Marriage.* New York: Alpha Books: A Division of Macmillan Reference USA, A Simon & Schuster Macmillan Company, 1997. The book has short chapters on lots of different topics related to marriage. At times, the book oversimplifies matters, but there are a few places in which it gives a nice summary on a particular topic.

Roiphe, Anne. *Married.* New York: Basic Books: A Member of the Perseus Books Group, 2002. A novelist's personal reflection on marriage. While not an academic work with references, there were a few valuable citations.

Satlow, Michael L. *Jewish Marriage in Antiquity.* Princeton, New Jersey: Princeton University Press, 2001. A study of marriage and its development in ancient Jewish communities. The book has information in three sections: 1. Thinking about Marriage, 2. Marrying, and 3. Staying Married.

Scarf, Maggie. *Intimate Partners.* New York: Random House, 1987. Approaches marriage from a "systems" approach, suggesting that marriage follows patterns established in previous generations. Scarf also suggests that couples unconsciously agree to certain behavior patterns for their union. The book was helpful in terms of directing thinking, if not for many citations.

Schnitzer, Jeshaia. "Marriages in Difficulty." *Marriage: An Interfaith Guide for All Couples.* Ed. Rev. Raban Hathorn, et al. New York: Association Press, 1970. 223–38. A book designed to give a "religious" view of marriage, but not from one particular religious perspective. An interesting idea, but the age of the book made it of limited use as the understanding of how to build a successful marriage has advanced considerably since then.

Simring, Steven, M.D., P.P.H. *Making Marriage Work for Dummies.* Foster City, CA: IDG Books Worldwide, 1999. A broad sweep of many important topics related to building a successful marriage. Much more information and better writing than the Idiot's Guide.

Stern, Ronald H. "The Talmudic Origins of Rabbinic Counseling." Diss. Rabbinical School, Hebrew Union College, 1990. Looks at the origins of counseling related to many subjects, including illness and death. There are a few places where the thesis discusses marriage and provided a few Talmudic references, but most of the thesis was outside the scope of this research.

Suchard, Tzadok Shmuel. *Making Your Marriage Work.* New York: Rabbi S. Suchard, 1981. A traditional account on building a successful marriage. Other traditional marriage guides proved more transferable to a liberal marriage manual.

Tannen, Ph.d., Deborah. *You Just Don't Understand.* New York: Ballantine Books, 1990. A popular book on the difference in communication between men and women.

Telushkin, Rabbi Joseph. *Jewish Wisdom.* New York: William Morrow and Company, Inc., 1994. A collection of Jewish texts on various topics from the ethical to the political.

Thorman, George. *Marriage Counseling Handbook.* Springfield, Illinois: Charles C. Thomas, 1996. A good resource for outlining the field of marriage counseling and different counseling approaches.

Travis, Rabbi Tsvi Dov. *The Jewish Marriage.* New York: Empire Press, 1985. A traditional account of marriage that provided a few interesting citations. Much of the book echoed other similar works read for this research.

A Treasury of Jewish Quotations. 1956. Ed. Joseph L. Baron. Northvale, New Jersey: Jason Aronson Inc., 1985. Contains quotes both ancient and modern on various topics, only a few of which were relevant to this project.

Venditti, M. D., Michael C. *How to Be Your Own Marriage Counselor.* New York: The Continuum Publishing Company, 1980. Written by a physician, this book is an interesting take on marriage. The writing was not stellar and some of the ideas were dated, but a physician's perspective was valuable.

Waldman, Mark Robert. *Love Games.* New York: Jeremy P. Tarcher/ Putnam a member of Penguin Putnam Inc., 2000. Uses games to approach potential conflict areas that relationships often face. Many of the games deal with meditation practice and the like. Not all the activities labeled as "games" seemed like games, but rather as vehicles to spark conversation.

Wallerstein, Judith S. and Blakeslee, Sandra. *The Good Marriage.* Boston: Houghton Mifflin Company, 1995. The author researched people who identified their marriages as "good." She posits that there are four kinds of marriage: romantic, rescue, companionate, and traditional. Some good information came out of this book.

Weiss, Ph.D, Rabbi Abner, licensed marriage and family therapist. "Marital Counseling." Stephen S. Wise Temple. The Board of Rabbis of Southern California. 10/March. 2003. A lecture given to a small seminar of members of the Pacific Association of Reform Rabbis by an experienced marriage counselor. Among other topics, the importance of mirroring (active listening), validation, and empathizing were stressed.

Westheimer, Dr. Ruth K. and Mark, Jonathan. *Heavenly Sex.* New York: The Continuum Publishing Company, 1995. This book was surprisingly useful. Dr. Ruth makes use of many Biblical and Talmudic sources.

Endnotes

1. Sharon S. Brehm, et al., *Intimate Relationships*, 3rd ed., 1985 (New York, NY: McGraw-Hill Higher Education, 2002), 27.
2. Daniel H. Bass, "Premarital Counseling," diss., Jewish Communal Service, Hebrew Union College, 1982, 15.
3. Robert M. Benjamin, "The Role of the Reform Rabbi in Premarital Counseling," diss., Rabbinical School, Hebrew Union College, 1966, 9.
4. *Pre-Marital Counseling*, ed. Rabbi David M. Feldman (New York: Commission on Synagogue Relations: Federation of Jewish Philanthropies of New York, 1974) 7.
5. Jeshaia Schnitzer, "Marriages in Difficulty," *Marriage: An Interfaith Guide for All Couples*, ed. Rev. Raban Hathorn, et al, (New York: Association Press, 1970), 235.
6. Brehm, et al., *Intimate Relationships*, 10.
7. David R. Mace, *Close Companions* (New York: The Continuum Publishing Company, 1982), 21.
8. Judith S. Wallerstein and Sandra Blakeslee, *The Good Marriage* (Boston: Houghton Mifflin Company, 1995), 5.
9. Anne Roiphe, *Married* (New York: Basic Books: A Member of the Perseus Books Group, 2002), 78.
10. Maggie Scarf, *Intimate Partners* (New York: Random House, 1987), 37.
11. Michael Kaufman, *Love, Marriage, and Family in Jewish Law and Tradition* (Northvale, New Jersey: Jason Aronson, Inc., 1992), 11.
12. Kaufman, *Love, Marriage, and Family in Jewish Law and Tradition*, 99.

13. Kaufman, *Love, Marriage, and Family in Jewish Law and Tradition,* 72.

14. Kaufman, *Love, Marriage, and Family in Jewish Law and Tradition,* 261.

15. Brehm, et al., *Intimate Relationships,* 244.

16. Bass, "Premarital Counseling," 67.

17. Benjamin, "The Role of the Reform Rabbi in Premarital Counseling," 20–21.

18. Rabbi Ellen Jay Lewis, "Preparing for the *Chupah:* Premarital Counseling," *Jewish Pastoral Care,* ed. Rabbi Dayle A. Friedman (Woodstock, Vermont: Jewish Lights Publishing, 2001), 207.

19. Wallerstein, *The Good Marriage,* 13.

20. Wallerstein, *The Good Marriage,* 184.

21. Kaufman, *Love, Marriage, and Family in Jewish Law and Tradition,* 119.

22. Steven Carr Reuben, *But How Will You Raise the Children?* (New York: Pocket Books, 1987), 130.

23. Cantors are also able to marry couples. For the sake of convenience, we will use rabbi to refer to the rabbi or cantor who is performing the wedding.

24. Anita Diamant, *The New Jewish Wedding* (New York: Fireside, 1985), 70.

25. Diamant, *The New Jewish Wedding,* 152.

26. Kahlil Gibran, *The Prophet* (New York: Alfred A. Knopf, 1923), 15.

27. Maurice Lamm, *The Jewish Way in Love and Marriage* (San Francisco: Harper & Row, Publishers, 1980), 188.

28. *The Rabbinical Assembly Rabbi's Manual* (New York: The Rabbinical Assembly, 1998), C-49–50.

29. Jewish weddings do not, traditionally, contain those famous lines from TV weddings, "Do you, so and so, take so and so to be your lawfully wedded husband/wife." This is because those promises were traditionally made in the *ketubah* that the groom signed.

30. Diamant, *The New Jewish Wedding,* 179.

31. Helen Latner, *The Everything Jewish Wedding Book* (Holbrook, Massachusetts: Adams Media Corporation, 1998), 82–3.

32. Dr. Ruth K. Westheimer and Jonathan Mark, *Heavenly Sex* (New York: The Continuum Publishing Company, 1995), 135.

33. Those who were raised by a single parent by choice or those who never met their second parent learn about marriage primarily from friends, family, and community.

34. William Betcher, M.D. and Robbie Macauley, *The Seven Basic Quarrels of Marriage* (Toronto: Random House, Inc., 1990), 15.

35. Mark Robert Waldman, *Love Games* (New York: Jeremy P. Tarcher/Putnam a member of Penguin Putnam Inc., 2000), 75–6.

36. Waldman, *Love Games,* 104–5, adapted.

37. Scarf, *Intimate Partners,* 88.

38. *The Jewish Marriage Anthology,* ed. Philip and Hanna Goodman, 1965 (Philadelphia: The Jewish Publication Society of America, 1971), 72–3.

39. Wallerstein and Blakeslee, *The Good Marriage,* 27–8.

40. Francine Klagsbrun, *Voices of Wisdom* (Middle Village, New York: Jonathan David Publishers, Inc., 1980), 121.

41. Betcher and Macauley, *The Seven Basic Quarrels of Marriage,* 63.

42. Westheimer and Mark, *Heavenly Sex,* 135.

43. Miriam Arond and Samuel L. Pauker, M.D., *The First Year of Marriage* (New York: Warner Books, 1987), 39.

44. M. Gary Neuman, *Emotional Infidelity* (New York: Crown Publishers, 2001), 285–6.

45. Reuben, *But How Will You Raise the Children?,* 76.

46. Gloria Call Horsley, RN, MFCC, *The In-Law Survival Manual* (New York: John Wiley & Sons, Inc., 1996), 233.

47. Steven Simring, M.D., P.P.H. and Sue Klavans Simring, D.S.W., *Making Marriage Work for Dummies* (Foster City, CA: IDG Books Worldwide, 1999), 160.

48. If this particular example doesn't apply to your family, ideally you can come up with an example appropriate to your family.

49. Willard F. Harley Jr., *Fall in Love Stay in Love* (Grand Rapids, Michigan: Fleming H. Revell, 2001), 120.

50. Brehm, et al., *Intimate Relationships,* 146.

51. Brehm, et al., *Intimate Relationships,* 339.

52. Waldman, *Love Games,* 138.

53. To structure the remainder of this section, I will use the model employed by those who compiled Medieval Jewish law books who stated the general rule and then showed how, as with any rule, there are exceptions and additional things to consider. To that end, please read the entire section before reacting or trying to put any of this information into practice.

54. Brehm, et al., *Intimate Relationships,* 351.

55. Kaufman, *Love, Marriage, and Family in Jewish Law and Tradition,* 251.

56.   As discussed in the introduction, some of the sources for this manual are drawn from ancient texts, and reflect the social circumstances of their times. We can still use these texts if we are willing to recognize that the message that they contain applies for any arrangement of partners.

57.   Kaufman, *Love, Marriage, and Family in Jewish Law and Tradition,* 259.

58.   Brehm, et al., *Intimate Relationships,* 141.

59.   Brehm, et al., *Intimate Relationships,* 131.

60.   Brehm, et al., *Intimate Relationships,* 135.

61.   Neuman, *Emotional Infidelity,* 187.

62.   John M. Gottman, Ph.D. and Nan Silver, *The Seven Principles for Making Marriage Work* (New York: Crown Publishers, Inc., 1999), 260–1.

63.   Brehm, et al., *Intimate Relationships,* 351.

64.   Kaufman, *Love, Marriage, and Family in Jewish Law and Tradition,* 59.

65.   Rabbi Aaron Landes, "Sample Interview: Jewish Marriage," *Pre-Marital Counseling,* ed. Rabbi David M. Feldman (New York: Commission on Synagogue Relations: Federation of Jewish Philanthropies of New York, 1974), 34.

66.   Mark Goulston, M.D. with Philip Goldberg, *The 6 Secrets of a Lasting Relationship* (New York: G. P. Putnam's Sons, 2001), 63.

67.   Kaufman, *Love, Marriage, and Family in Jewish Law and Tradition,* 110.

68.   Goulston and Goldberg, *The 6 Secrets of a Lasting Relationship,* 30.

69.   Goulston and Goldberg, *The 6 Secrets of a Lasting Relationship,* 117–8.

70.   Waldman, *Love Games,* 41.

71.   Hilary Rich and Helama Laks Kravitz, M.D., *The Complete Idiot's Guide to the Perfect Marriage* (New York: Alpha Books: A Division of Macmillan Reference USA, A Simon & Schuster Macmillan Company, 1997), 42–3.

72.   Brehm, et al., *Intimate Relationships,* 147–8.

73.   abbi Shlomo Aviner, *Dimensions of Love* (Jerusalem: Urim Publications, 2000), 188.

74.   Betcher and Macauley, *The Seven Basic Quarrels of Marriage,* 162.

75.   Mace, *Close Companions,* 86.

76. Kaufman, *Love, Marriage, and Family in Jewish Law and Tradition*, 268.

77. David R. Mace, *Getting Ready for Marriage* (Nashville: Abingdon Press, 1972), 72.

78. *Domestic Abuse Statistics*. 24/Feb. 2004 <http://www.chaicolorado.org/statistics.htm>.

79. Jennifer Karotkin, *Press Release: JWI Publications Setting the Standard for Discussion of Domestic Abuse in the Jewish Community*. 23/September 2002 <http://www.jewishwomen.org/press/2002/0923.htm>.

80. Harley, *Fall in Love Stay in Love*, 201.

81. *The Jewish Marriage Anthology*, 47. Quotation is from Israel ibn Al-nakawa (?–1391) of Spain.

82. Kaufman, *Love, Marriage, and Family in Jewish Law and Tradition*, 34. Quotation is from Zohar Hadash, Genesis 5.

83. Waldman, *Love Games*, 97–8, adapted.

84. Betcher and Macauley, *The Seven Basic Quarrels of Marriage*, 99.

85. Kaufman, *Love, Marriage, and Family in Jewish Law and Tradition*, 253.

86. Harley, *Fall in Love Stay in Love*, 44.

87. Waldman, *Love Games*, 56.

88. Goulston and Goldberg, *The 6 Secrets of a Lasting Relationship*, 173, adapted.

89. Waldman, *Love Games*, 91.

90. Rich and Kravitz, *The Complete Idiot's Guide to the Perfect Marriage*, 272.

91. Brehm, et al., *Intimate Relationships*, 219–24, 232–33.

92. Lamm, *The Jewish Way in Love and Marriage*, 122.

93. Aviner. *Dimensions of Love*, 68.

94. Kaufman, *Love, Marriage, and Family in Jewish Law and Tradition*, 97.

95. *The Jewish Marriage Anthology*, 29.

96. Kaufman, *Love, Marriage, and Family in Jewish Law and Tradition*, 278.

97. Mace, *Close Companions*, 188.

98. Dr. Melvyn Kinder and Dr. Connell Cowan, *Husbands and Wives* (New York: Clarkson N. Potter, Inc., 1989), 138.

99. Blakeslee and Wallerstein, *The Good Marriage*, 155.

100. 100. Brehm, et al., *Intimate Relationships*, 178–206.

101. Miriam Around and Samuel L. Pauker, M.D., *The First Year of Marriage* (New York: Warner Books, 1987), 213.

102. Brehm, et al., *Intimate Relationships,* 264.

103. Brehm, et al., *Intimate Relationships,* 265.

104. Roland B. Gittelsohn, *The Extra Dimension* (New York: Union of American Hebrew Congregations, 1983), 102.

105. Brehm, et al., *Intimate Relationships,* 268.

106. *The Jewish Marriage Anthology,* 292.

107. Kaufman, *Love, Marriage, and Family in Jewish Law and Tradition,* 116.

108. Gittelsohn, *The Extra Dimension,* 133.

109. Yitzhak Buxbaum, *Jewish Spiritual Practices* (Northvale, New Jersey: Jason Aronson, Inc., 1990), 591.

110. Rabbi Michael Gold, *Does God Belong in the Bedroom?* (Philadelphia: The Jewish Publication Society, 1992), 3–4.

111. Aviner, *Dimensions of Love,* 24.

112. Gold, *Does God Belong in the Bedroom?,* 22.

113. Kaufman, *Love, Marriage, and Family in Jewish Law and Tradition,* 199.

114. Brehm, et al., *Intimate Relationships,* 29.

115. Brehm, et al., *Intimate Relationships,* 288.

116. Rich and Kravitz, *The Complete Idiot's Guide to the Perfect Marriage,* 241.

117. Scarf, *Intimate Partners,* 133.

118. Wallerstein and Blakeslee, *The Good Marriage,* 258.

119. Mace, *Getting Ready for Marriage,* 111–2.

120. Waldman, *Love Games,* 108.

121. Kaufman, *Love, Marriage, and Family in Jewish Law and Tradition,* 5.

122. Kaufman, *Love, Marriage, and Family in Jewish Law and Tradition,* 4–5.

123. It is possible for those who choose not to have children or are unable to have them to participate in this *mitzvah*. Jewish tradition says that "your children" can also be "your students."

124. Brehm, et al., *Intimate Relationships,* 173.

125. Robert Gordis, *Love & Sex* (New York: Farrar Straus Giroux, 1978), 100.

126. Azriella Jaffe, *Two Jews Can Still Be a Mixed Marriage* (Franklin Lakes, New Jersey: Career Press, 2000), 3.

127. Dr. Paul Coleman, *The 30 Secrets of Happily Married Couples* (Holbrook, MA: Bob Adams, Inc., 1992), 139.

128. Gittelsohn, *The Extra Dimension,* 245.
129. Rabbi Alan S. Green, *Sex, God, and the Sabbath* (Cleveland: Temple Emanu El, 1979), 47–8.
130. Waldman, *Love Games,* 100–1, adapted.
131. Reuben, *But How Will You Raise the Children?,* 49, 61 adapted.
132. Paul Cowan with Rachel Cowan, *Mixed Blessings* (New York: Doubleday, 1987), 247–8.
133. Reuben, *But How Will You Raise the Children?,* 202.
134. Michael L. Satlow, *Jewish Marriage in Antiquity* (Princeton, New Jersey: Princeton University Press, 2001), 43.
135. Aviner, *Dimensions of Love,* 53- 4.
136. Lamm, *The Jewish Way in Love and Marriage,* 162.
137. Lamm, *The Jewish Way in Love and Marriage,* 163.
138. Kaufman, *Love, Marriage, and Family in Jewish Law and Tradition,* 30.

About the Author

Rabbi Daniel Young was ordained at Hebrew Union College in Los Angeles in 2004. He wrote his rabbinical thesis on the topic of premarital counseling and has counseled many couples preparing for marriage. He and his wife Beth live in Miami, where they continually strive to infuse their own marriage with meaning.